The Making of a Patriot

....

Critical Historical Encounters

Series Editors
James Kirby Martin
David M. Oshinsky
Randy W. Roberts

Frank Lambert *The Battle of Ole Miss: Civil Rights v. States' Rights*
Sheila L. Skemp *The Making of a Patriot: Benjamin Franklin at the Cockpit*

The Making of a Patriot

....

Benjamin Franklin at the Cockpit

SHEILA L. SKEMP

OXFORD
UNIVERSITY PRESS

OXFORD
UNIVERSITY PRESS

Oxford University Press, Inc., publishes works that further
Oxford University's objective of excellence
in research, scholarship, and education.

Oxford   New York
Auckland   Cape Town   Dar es Salaam   Hong Kong   Karachi
Kuala Lumpur   Madrid   Melbourne   Mexico City   Nairobi
New Delhi   Shanghai   Taipei   Toronto

With offices in
Argentina   Austria   Brazil   Chile   Czech Republic   France   Greece
Guatemala   Hungary   Italy   Japan   Poland   Portugal   Singapore
South Korea   Switzerland   Thailand   Turkey   Ukraine   Vietnam

Published by Oxford University Press, Inc.
198 Madison Avenue, New York, New York 10016
www.oup.com

Oxford is a registered trademark of Oxford University Press

Library of Congress Cataloging-in-Publication Data
Skemp, Sheila L.
The making of a patriot : Benjamin Franklin at the Cockpit / Sheila L. Skemp.—1st ed.
    p.   cm.—(Critical Historical Encounters)
ISBN 978-0-19-538657-8 (hardcover : alk. paper)—ISBN 978-0-19-538656-1
(pbk. : alk. paper)
1. Franklin, Benjamin, 1706–1790. 2. Statesmen—United States—Biography.
3. United States—History—Revolution, 1775–1783—Causes. 4. Rosslyn, Alexander Wedderburn,
Earl of, 1733–1805. 5. Royal Cockpit (Whitehall, London, England) I. Title.
E302.6.F8S63   2012
973.3092—dc23   [B]   2011038772

1 3 5 7 9 8 6 4 2

Printed in the United States of America
on acid-free paper

To Murphy

CONTENTS

....

EDITORS' FOREWORD

....

The volumes in this Oxford University Press book series focus on major critical encounters in the American experience. The word "critical" refers to formative, vital, transforming events and actions that have had a major impact in shaping the ever-changing contours of life in the United States. "Encounter" indicates a confrontation or clash, oftentimes but not always contentious in character, but always full of profound historical meaning and consequence.

In this framework, the United States, it can be said, has evolved on contested ground. Conflict and debate, the clash of peoples and ideas, have marked and shaped American history. The first Europeans transported with them cultural assumptions that collided with Native American values and ideas. Africans forced into bondage and carried to America added another set of cultural beliefs that often were at odds with those of Native Americans and Europeans. Over the centuries America's diverse peoples differed on many issues, often resulting in formative conflict that in turn gave form and meaning to the American experience.

The Critical Historical Encounters series emphasizes formative episodes in America's contested history. Each volume contains two fundamental ingredients: a carefully written narrative of the encounter and the consequences, both immediate and long-term, of that moment of conflict in America's contested history.

The era of the American Revolution represents one of those crucially important determinative periods in U.S. history. As relations between the British imperial government and the American colonists deteriorated, all colonists faced a personal crisis. They had to decide whether to rebel, remain loyal, or tread a middle course of neutrality with the hope that the looming war would not disrupt their lives.

No colonist was better known in the British imperial world than the brilliantly creative Benjamin Franklin. His origins were humble, but he used his immense talents to become a significant political leader in Pennsylvania, leading to his controversial service as an agent representing colonial interests in London, the seat of Empire. In many ways, Franklin loved being a part of the British world. He was not the kind of person who had a natural rebel's temperament. But then something went wrong for him. His attitude toward the Empire changed dramatically, and he emerged as a major leader of the American Revolution.

Along with so many other colonial Americans, Franklin, once so proud to be a British subject, had to reckon with his own political allegiance. Like hundreds of thousands of other colonists, his decision represented a critical personal encounter, based on his particular experiences with the issues, events, and personalities of his era. The reasons for Franklin's decision were unique to him, but they also personified what others went through as they faced the often traumatic process of whether to renounce their long-standing political allegiance to the mighty British Empire.

Historian Sheila Skemp engagingly explores Benjamin Franklin's story about how he became a Revolutionary while also reflecting on Franklin's son William, the last royal governor of New Jersey, who chose to remain loyal to the British Crown. The Revolution did divide families and friends in what was both a creative and hurtful process, not only for the Franklins but for every colonist who lived during that turbulent era and who witnessed, in the end, the formation of a new, independent republic among the nations of the world. The subject of Benjamin Franklin's allegiance is at the core of that compelling story.

PREFACE

....

On January 29, 1774, Benjamin Franklin appeared before a raucous group of Englishmen in a room in Whitehall Palace known as the Cockpit. Most members of the Privy Council, a select group of the King's advisors, were present. Other notables also managed to crowd into the tiny room. For a little over an hour, Franklin stood silently as he was subjected to a vicious harangue at the hands of Solicitor General Alexander Wedderburn. Wedderburn's audience loved it. They laughed and clapped and jeered as Franklin's tormenter hurled one verbal blow after another at his unfortunate victim. Franklin had been living in London for nearly a decade, serving as a colonial agent or lobbyist for Pennsylvania and three other colonies. During that time, he had met and worked with many of the men who now took such pleasure in his humiliation. He loved England, was comfortable in the nation's capital, and had done all he could to strengthen the bonds of Empire. As late as January 5—nineteen days before his appearance at the Cockpit—he was continuing his efforts to arrive at what he characterized as "an accommodation of our differences." Only after January 29 did Franklin decide that such an accommodation was impossible to achieve. The confrontation at the Cockpit had inadvertently turned one of the King's most loyal and dependable subjects into one of England's most determined enemies.

This book is not a traditional biography. It makes no effort to take its readers step by step through Franklin's long and distinguished career. Instead, it focuses on one, critical moment in Benjamin Franklin's life. It describes the series of events that led Franklin to the Cockpit as well as the ramifications of his experience for himself, for the colonies he served, and for the Empire he venerated. At every point along the way, it reminds readers that Franklin's ultimate decision to lend his support to those men and women who hoped to destroy the ties that bound the colonies to England was by no means a foregone conclusion. Franklin was, until very late in the game, a proud "Empire man" at the very time when radicals in England and America were moving ever closer to the brink of war. The road that led Franklin— and indeed most Americans—to opt for independence was filled with torturous twists and turns. That road ended at the Cockpit.

Although most of Franklin's biographers at least mention the Cockpit incident and grant its importance, none has put that incident front and center; none has looked at the larger meaning it had. This book is designed to do just that. It provides readers with a micro history that focuses on Franklin, one of the most well-known leaders of the patriot movement. At the same time, it serves as a macro history that provides insights on the colonial decision to move, as historian Pauline Maier has put it, "from resistance to revolution." Looked at from one perspective, then, Franklin's experience is simply the story of the decision of one man—albeit a very important man—to renounce his loyalty to King and country. But Franklin's story, unique in so many ways, can be read as emblematic of the process by which colonists everywhere moved slowly and with considerable trepidation toward independence. Viewing the coming of the Revolution through the lens of Franklin's experience, readers will be able to appreciate the difficult process by which British-Americans became, simply, Americans.

In as much as this book focuses on Franklin, it does something else. It helps readers come to grips with the complexities of a man who is arguably the most beloved, the most disparaged, and the least understood of America's founders. Both his detractors and his admirers characterize Franklin as the quintessential representative American. Some see his life as the classic rags-to-riches story and argue that his ability to rise from his humble origins to the loftiest of heights proves that America is and always has been the land of opportunity. Others stress his apparent pragmatism, his predilection for compromise, his determination to achieve the possible rather than tilt at windmills. For those who disdain Franklin—and are often critical of the very American values that he supposedly represents—Franklin is little more than that "snuff-colored man" made so famous by D.H. Lawrence. He is smug, pompous, self-satisfied, the ultimate bourgeois. In either rendition, however, Franklin the human being is reduced to a caricature. Franklin deserves so much more than that. He was more cosmopolitan and less "American" than most of the founders. He was at least as emotional as he was rational. He was capable of anger and joy, ambition and frustration, brilliance and ruthlessness. And his experience at the Cockpit brought all of his very human emotions to the fore.

This book begins with a discussion of the experience at the Cockpit, an event that not only moved Franklin once and for all into the patriot camp but presaged the beginning of the end of England's control of its mainland colonies. It describes the events that took place in January of 1774. It then examines the complex set of circumstances that led to those events and it analyzes Franklin's reaction to his experience in the days and months that followed. Occurring as it did, in the immediate aftermath of what later became known as the "Boston Tea Party" and right before Parliament passed its infamous Coercive Acts, the timing of the Cockpit incident clearly occurred at a crucial—some would say providential—time. His humiliation at the hands of Alexander Wedderburn was a personal turning point for Franklin. Never again did he trust the King's men to do the right thing; never again was he willing to compromise with officials who did not seem willing to meeting him even halfway. It took most colonists two years to catch up with Franklin. Nevertheless, by 1774 it was becoming increasingly clear to some that the gap between England and its colonies had grown too wide to close. This, then, was a seminal time, a defining moment— for Franklin *and* for America.

The remaining chapters analyze the ramifications of the Cockpit incident from a variety of thematic perspectives. One chapter examines the very impressive cast of characters present, or "virtually present" in Whitehall on January 29. Others deal with the "causes" of the Revolution, using the Cockpit as a jumping-off point. Taken together, they argue that what looks from hindsight to be a steady march toward independence and "democracy," was in fact neither inevitable nor preordained. They also do a great deal to demystify a man who has assumed almost iconic stature in the minds of most Americans. Finally, the book looks at the ramifications of the Cockpit incident on Franklin's own family. A discussion of the division between Benjamin Franklin and his son William, the royal governor of New Jersey, reminds readers that not all colonists were Patriots, and that the American Revolution was not only a war for independence but a civil war, a war that divided father and son, brother and sister, neighbor and friend.

Benjamin Franklin understood the complexities of the world in which he lived better than most people—then and even now—were able to do. Consequently he was less likely than most to view his circumstances as a simple fight between good and evil. Perhaps for that very reason, he was reluctant to argue that English leaders, many of whom he knew personally, were bent on subjugating the colonies, nor did he view all colonists through rose-colored glasses. He knew that neither the men who ruled the Empire nor the Americans who resisted that rule were perfect. They stumbled, they blundered, they fell. But who didn't? Mere mortals could be expected to fail at times, but Franklin knew from first hand experience that humans could learn from even their worst mistakes. And thus, until 1774, he was content to soldier on, looking for ways to bring Englishmen and colonists closer together. After 1774, however, he no longer felt that reform of the Empire and its leaders was possible. And if that was the case, independence was not only desirable; it was necessary.

I have enjoyed the support of a number of people as I prepared this book for publication. Above all, James Kirby Martin, the editor of this series, has offered me sage advice in a variety of ways. Whether he was commenting on the substance of each chapter or my on own occasional infelicities of phrase, Jim's observations have always been right on target. I have shared portions of this manuscript with two groups of scholars: the Delta Women Writers; and a less organized, interdisciplinary group centered at the University of Mississippi, whose members all study the "long eighteenth century." The response to my drafts from both groups was critical in the best sense of the term. The services and guidance of Brian Wheel and Sarah Ellerton at Oxford University Press have been invaluable. Finally, I am especially grateful to the reviewers of my completed manuscript: Kathryn Braund, Auburn University; Rory T. Cornish, Winthrop University; Jennifer Dorsey, Siena College; Sara S. Gronim, Long Island University; Steven C. Hahn, St. Olaf College; Greg O'Malley, University of California,

Santa Cruz; David A Raney, Hillsdale College; Walter Sargent, University of Maine, Farmington; Matthew Schoenbachler, University of North Alabama; Andrew Shankman, Rutgers University; and John Smolenski, University of California, Davis. These folks were amazing. They read the manuscript with care, criticized it, suggested ways to improve it, and even caught a few typos! I hope that all of them will see at least some evidence that I have looked at their comments with the seriousness that they surely deserve.

CHAPTER 1

....

The Cockpit

On January 29, 1774 Benjamin Franklin walked out of a tiny room in Whitehall Palace known as the "Cockpit." The room had a long and storied history. Built by Henry VIII in 1530, it had been the scene of cockfights for nearly half a century before it was converted into a theater and then occupied by the Board of the Treasury. As he left the scene, Franklin must have felt as though the powers that be had decided to return the facility to its original purpose, and that he, rather than some unfortunate barnyard fowl, had just endured a ritual sacrifice at the hands of a foe who had every advantage over him. He watched in disbelief as well wishers gathered around Solicitor General Alexander Wedderburn, a man young enough to be his son, who had just subjected him to so public a humiliation. He could not help but wince as jubilant admirers slapped Wedderburn on the back, shook his hand, and offered him their heartiest congratulations for a job well done. How, he wondered, had it come to this? How had one of England's most loyal American subjects found himself standing before the king's advisers, vilified as a dangerous rabble rouser intent upon colonial independence?

Franklin had entered the west side of Whitehall Palace a little less than an hour earlier. Clad in a decidedly old-fashioned wig and a simple blue coat of Manchester velvet, he knew that his sartorial efforts did not impress many in the overflow crowd. Most members of the Privy Council (the king's chief advisory body) were able to secure seats at a mammoth table that stretched from one end of the octagonal-shaped room to the other. Everyone else, including sixty-eight-year-old Benjamin Franklin, had to remain standing during the entire ordeal. The audience was a veritable who's who of London's most important—in some cases most self-important—men. Thirty-five Privy Councilors showed up for the festivities, as did such notables as General Thomas Gage, philosopher Jeremy Bentham, scientist Joseph Priestley, member of Parliament Edmund Burke, and Lord North, King George III's chief minister.

Under ordinary circumstances, Franklin's appearance at the Cockpit would have raised no eyebrows, drawn no crowds. It would have been a routine affair. Franklin was there in his capacity as agent (a combination lobbyist and ambassador) for the colony of Massachusetts. He had been summoned there to defend a petition from the Bay Colony's legislature asking for the removal of Governor Thomas Hutchinson and Lieutenant Governor Andrew Oliver from their respective posts. Much to Franklin's dismay, what in less rancorous

Christian Schussele, *Franklin Before the Privy Council in the Cockpit*, 1774.
Courtesy of the Huntington Art Collections, San Marino, California.

times would have been a mere formality was about to be transformed into high political theater.

The timing of the hearing could not have been worse. All of London had just heard the news of events in Boston. On December 16, 1773 a group of colonists, for some unfathomable reason disguised as Indians, had boarded three ships in Boston Harbor and had thrown the precious cargo—tea belonging to the British East India Company—into the water. This audacious destruction of private property was calculated to infuriate all London officialdom. Since the end of the Seven Years' War in 1763, the colonial legislatures, usually known as assemblies, had been locked in a battle with Parliament over their respective rights and duties. The colonists insisted that only their individual assemblies could tax them. They held that Parliament could not tax its mainland possessions because Americans had no representation in that august body. Parliament could not imagine that its power could be limited by anyone, even the king, surely not by inferior provincial governments. Again and again the two forces had clashed. Parliament would devise new ways to secure revenue from its colonies. The colonies invariably protested each innovation— usually, or so it seemed, led by Massachusetts—petitioned the king for redress, and eventually refused to purchase goods coming from England. Occasionally violence broke out. Those colonists who so much as appeared to support parliamentary prerogative watched helplessly as well-organized mobs destroyed their homes, warehouses, and shops. In the end, Parliament always backed down, insisting that it did so voluntarily and that it had never relinquished its right to tax. And each time the government sounded even a partial retreat, hardliners warned that lawmakers were simply postponing the inevitable, encouraging American "rebels," and sending the signal that Parliament did not have the fortitude to enforce its own laws. What became known as the "Boston Tea Party" was proof positive, to all but the most confident Englishmen, that the doomsayers had been right all along. Angry, frustrated, even a little hurt, English officials were out for blood. They were looking for someone to blame for all the ills that were besetting the English Empire. Benjamin Franklin was a convenient target.

When the king received the Massachusetts Assembly's request for the removal of Hutchinson and Oliver, he referred the matter to the Privy Council for its consideration and advice. Although Franklin had hoped that George III would simply reject the petition without a hearing, he was not especially surprised by the king's decision, nor did he seem unduly concerned.[1] He was puzzled, but still not worried, when he received a summons from the council on January 8 requiring his presence three days later. Knowing full well that the petition was "not likely to be complied with," he continued to assume that the Privy Council would dispose of the matter quickly. Still, he forged ahead, going through the motions to prepare his defense of the Bay Colony's request.[2]

Thus Franklin was caught completely off guard when he learned on the eve of the hearing that Governor Hutchinson's representative in London, Israel Mauduit, had received permission to be represented by counsel. Mauduit claimed, somewhat disingenuously, that he feared "Dr. Franklin's great abilities" and did not want to put his client at a disadvantage.[3] Somewhat taken aback by this unexpected turn of events, Franklin decided that he, too, should seek counsel, and so he begged for a postponement of the hearing. His request was granted. The hearing would take place on January 29 instead of on the eleventh.[4] Franklin's success in this small matter turned out to be a Pyrrhic victory. News of the destruction of the tea in Boston Harbor arrived in London on January 20, just nine days before his appearance at the Cockpit. Already irritated by Franklin's increasingly pointed attacks in the press, pieces that even their author conceded were a little "saucy," and furious at what they saw as the insolence of the Massachusetts Assembly, the members of the Privy Council were more determined than ever to find someone to blame for the troubles that roiled the Empire.[5] What had begun as a routine meeting of the king's advisers had become a more serious affair than anyone would have imagined possible just a few months earlier.

Even before he walked into the Cockpit Franklin was prepared for what he later described as a "Bull-baiting."[6] He knew perfectly well that the news of the "transactions relating to the tea had increased and strengthened the torrent of clamour" against the colonies. Moreover, he had been warned by those who claimed to be in the know that the hearing's outcome was a foregone conclusion. Many Londoners were convinced that he had helped put in motion the events that resulted in the Tea Party and that he bore the lion's share of the responsibility for the bad blood that existed between Governor Hutchinson and the

Massachusetts Assembly. Thus, the Privy Council had already determined that Franklin's reputation would be "blackened" and that the petition would "be rejected with some epithets, the assembly to be censured, and some honour done the governours."[7] That Solicitor General Alexander Wedderburn would be representing Hutchinson's interests was further evidence that things would not go well for either Franklin or the Massachusetts petition.

A native of Scotland, Wedderburn moved to London in the mid-1750s. From that time on he worked diligently to erase any remaining vestiges of provincialism that clung to him, even hiring a tutor to help him get rid of his accent. Called to the bar in 1757, he rose quickly through the ranks of the capital city's legal and political circles. Unabashedly ambitious, he forged connections—and made enemies—everywhere. He also married the sole child and heiress of John Dawson of Marly in Yorkshire, a union that added considerably to his already ample income. Most politicians knew Wedderburn as a man who easily altered his views to suit the prevailing winds. He had been an "extravagant" opponent of Lord North, for instance, until the offer of a better post led him to become one of the administration's firm supporters.[8] Similarly, he was a champion of rabble rouser John Wilkes in 1768, but a few years later he was on the opposite side. King George found his behavior more than a little suspicious, commenting on the "duplicity" that seemed to characterize Wedderburn's every move. He noted that "anyone that has carefully attended to the whole of that gentleman's political walk must see that he is not guided by principle, that self-conceit and what he thinks is his momentary interest alone sways him."[9]

Despite his character defects, no one denied that Wedderburn was an excellent orator. Some wryly referred to his "ubiquitous eloquence," while others—perhaps more flattering—thought he could make "the ministry's worst measures seem virtuous" by the sheer force of his arguments.[10] Most observers were convinced that it was Wedderburn's oratorical skills that had led North to dangle the solicitor general's position in front of him so as to woo him away from the opposition. The chief minister had been successful, and thus he was able to enjoy Wedderburn's performance—surely one of his finest—as he eviscerated Benjamin Franklin.

Franklin's lawyer, John Dunning, was also well known in London's legal circles but a temporary "disorder on his lungs" weakened his voice, making it virtually impossible for many in the room to hear him. He would not have been able to compete with Wedderburn's rhetoric in any case.[11] Dunning focused on what purported to be the issue at hand, the Massachusetts petition for the removal of Thomas Hutchinson and Andrew Oliver. He pointed out that the assembly had every right to petition the king. Moreover, no governor should—or even could—serve either king or colony if he was "obnoxious" to the people. Both Franklin and Dunning knew, of course, that what was considered "obnoxious" in Massachusetts would be seen in England "as virtues and merits." And so they had decided not to make any effort to prove that Hutchinson had actually done anything wrong. Instead, they contended that the petition itself was proof of the colonists' unhappiness. Indeed, there would have been no petition had there not been a complete breakdown in trust between assembly and governor.[12]

Then it was Wedderburn's turn to speak. It quickly became clear that the solicitor general's reputation for using words as weapons was well earned. In a personal, often scurrilous attack, he spoke for nearly an hour to the obvious delight of most in the audience. He was, observed General Gage, "serious, pathetick, and severe by turns: and I suppose no man's conduct and character was before so mangled and torn as Dr. Franklin's was at this time."[13] Pounding on the table for emphasis, Wedderburn began with an emotional defense of Governor Thomas Hutchinson. "No other man," he insisted, "could have been named, in whom so many favourable circumstances concurred to recommend him." Hutchinson was born and bred in Massachusetts, and he had served both colony and king in a variety of posts over the years. He had always behaved with integrity, even when doing so risked the loss of friends and property. Wedderburn mocked the pretensions of the Massachusetts Assembly "in a manner so ludicrous as to set the room in a loud laugh." And he insisted that it would be unjust to deprive Hutchinson of his position on the basis of "mere surmises." If the inhabitants of the Bay Colony could not accept this man as their governor, he asked rhetorically, was there any one in the British Empire who could hope to earn their trust?[14]

Wedderburn quickly disposed of the issue that was supposedly the purpose of the hearing. But a defense of Hutchinson and to a lesser extent of Oliver was not nearly enough—indeed it was not even the solicitor's main objective. His underlying argument was soon clear. Benjamin Franklin, he proclaimed, was part of a small but dangerous group of colonial agitators and demagogues who were determined to destroy the Empire. Franklin, he said, was one of the leading members of this "secret cabal." He was the "first mover and prime conductor," the "actor and secret spring," the "inventor and first planner" of the "secret designs" to achieve colonial independence. It was he, knowing that the Massachusetts Assembly was already "watching for any pretence to abuse and insult their Governors," who had used "fraudulent and corrupt means" to discredit Hutchinson, thus turning the unwitting people of Massachusetts against their honorable leader. Worse, he had managed to achieve his "most malignant of purposes." Thanks to Franklin, a "true incendiary," and his minions "the whole province [was] set in flame." The consequence, if England took no measures to stop the conspiracy in its tracks, would be the end of good government and the beginning of confusion and anarchy. Under the circumstances, Benjamin Franklin had "forfeited all the respect of societies and of men."[15] Indeed, in a remark designed to hurt Franklin's pride as much as anything he said, Wedderburn insinuated that Franklin was not even a legitimate agent. He moved "in a very inferior orbit," and he was merely the creature of men who "had their own private separate views" and were using their paid agitator for their own wicked purposes.[16]

On and on he went. By any standard it was a spectacular performance. Most of the audience loved it. Virtually all of Franklin's detractors but a decorous Lord North hooted and applauded as Wedderburn, in one observer's words, poured "forth such a torrent of virulent abuse on Dr. Franklin as never took place within the compass of my knowledge of judicial proceedings, his reproaches appearing to me incompatible with the principles of law, truth, justice, propriety, and humanity."[17] And through it all, Franklin said absolutely nothing, remaining silent, enduring the "invective and ribaldry" hurled at him, thinking that a common criminal would not have been subject to the treatment that he received in the Cockpit. He stood, said a sympathetic Edward Bancroft, "conspicuously erect, without the smallest movement of any part of his body." Even his facial expression did not change "during the continuance of the speech in which he was so harshly and improperly treated." He received Wedderburn's "thunder," observed a reporter from the *Public Advertiser*, "with philosophic

Tranquility and sovereign Contempt, whilst the approving Smiles of those at the Board clearly shew'd that the coarcest Language can be grateful to the politest Ears."[18] Franklin kept expecting someone to intervene, to point out that Wedderburn had ranged far from the topic at hand, that the Massachusetts agent was at the Cockpit only as a messenger delivering an entirely legal petition to the king, and that his own character—at least on this day—was irrelevant. But no one said a single word to stop the abuse.[19] Finally it was over. Wedderburn sat down. He invited his victim to respond, but Franklin "declared by his counsel, that he did not chuse to be examined."[20] There was nothing more to say.

The Privy Council's immediate decision to reject the Massachu-setts Assembly's petition was a predictable anticlimax. The council found the petition "inflammatory and precipitate." And it reiterated Wedderburn's argument that Benjamin Franklin was to blame for the distrust that poisoned the relationship between Massachusetts and England. Like Wedderburn, the members of the council believed that it was only the determination of a few dishonorable men to keep up "a Spirit of Clamour and Discontent" in Massachusetts that had led to the assembly's petition.[21] No one appeared to realize that they had in so short a time made an enemy of a man who longed to remain their friend.

Some of what happened to Benjamin Franklin on that fateful January day was beyond his control. As a colonial agent he had no choice but to defend a petition he had no hand in writing. Moreover, the news about the Tea Party arrived in London at the most inopportune time. But Franklin was not simply an innocent bystander caught in the crossfire between two increasingly antagonistic adversaries. He was as responsible as anyone at the Cockpit for a debacle that destroyed his reputation in England and moved the colonies one step closer to independence.

In the aftermath of the Tea Party, it was easy for many observers to forget that Franklin's ordeal had been precipitated not only by Bos-ton's destruction of the tea but also by a prolonged and ever-escalating quarrel between Thomas Hutchinson and the Massachusetts Assem-bly. Indeed, the lower house had sent its petition to London asking for the removal of Hutchinson and Oliver before the Tea Act was even on the books. Animosities between Hutchinson and the Bay Colony's legislators had been building up for a decade or more, although they had reached a crescendo in 1772. For over a year the Massachusetts legislature and Governor Hutchinson had been at loggerheads over their differing interpretations of Parliament's authority. The quarrel had begun when the assembly objected to plans hatched by Lord North's administration to grant royal governors an independent salary. It was not long before the governor and the assembly were engaged in verbal fisticuffs. The Bay Colony's lawmakers argued that they had the sole right to levy money for the support of their own government. Hutchinson insisted that Parliament's power could not be limited and that colonial legislatures were subordinate to lawmakers in London. In the end, frustrated by what it conceived as the governor's obstinacy, the House sent its ill-fated petition to the king. It was the unhappy duty of the Bay Colony agent to see that the petition received a proper hearing. Franklin never had any illusions about the petition's reception. Indeed, he thought it might well do more harm than good. Still, he had a job to do, and he did it. Thus, he brought the petition to Lord Dartmouth who was both the president of the Board of Trade (along with the Privy Council, one of the most important agencies devoted to colonial affairs) and the secretary of state for the American Department.

As objectionable as the assembly petition may have been, it was the colonial reaction to the Tea Act that led most English leaders to condemn first Massachusetts and eventually the colonies as a whole. As Franklin saw it, Lord North's administration was responsible for a piece of legislation that signaled the beginning of the end of Anglo-American unity as well as the termination of the long and tortured relationship between Governor Thomas Hutchinson and the colony of Massachusetts. Parliament set the wheels in motion as a result of the very real financial difficulties faced by the East India Company. The Company's troubles were in large measure a product of its own ineptitude and corruption, which resulted in declining income and rising costs. But it was also true that East India tea was rotting in London warehouses because many Americans were refusing to buy it. Some colonists simply preferred to purchase cheaper tea, most of which was smuggled into their ports by Dutch merchants. Others acted on principle, protesting the tax on tea that had been on the books since 1767 when the Townshend Acts had levied duties on certain luxury items that the colonists imported from England. Parliament had repealed most of the Townshend Duties in 1770, but the duty on tea remained, primarily as a symbol of England's right to tax the colonies. As a result, many colonists would not buy East India tea. By 1772 the Company was in desperate straits. It was not even able to pay annual dividends to its stockholders (many of whom were members of Parliament). Something clearly had to be done.

At first, Franklin saw the Company's difficulties as an opportunity. He was convinced that Parliament would have to repeal the tax on tea in an effort to persuade the colonists to drop their boycott. The East India Company agreed, even submitting a petition to Parliament to that effect.[22] Instead, in the spring of 1773, North pushed through— with only token opposition—what became known as the Tea Act.

North saw the act, which was to a great extent his own creation, as a brilliant solution to the Company's problems. It streamlined the process of bringing tea to the colonies, hence cutting costs at nearly every step of the way. It granted the Company a colonial monopoly, allowing it to use its own hand-picked agents to market its goods. It also gave the Company permission to send its tea directly to the colonies without first going through England, saving both time and money. Finally, it abolished the export duty on tea collected in English ports whenever the Company did send tea from England to America. When some suggested that Parliament should also abolish the tea tax collected in colonial ports, however, North balked. He assumed that most colonists would gladly buy tea that had suddenly become much cheaper and thus the government would reap a sizeable revenue from the taxes it collected. That money could be used to pay the salaries of colonial officials like Thomas Hutchinson, thereby reducing the power of the purse enjoyed by the increasingly obstreperous assemblies. Most gratifying, North would accomplish all this without retreating from Parliament's determination to maintain its right to tax the colonies.

North, of course, miscalculated. Many colonial merchants objected to the Tea Act because the Company's designated agents enjoyed a monopoly on the sale of East India tea, cutting all other entrepreneurs out of potential profits. They were especially angry in Massachusetts when they learned that Governor Thomas Hutchinson's two sons were the Company's principal consignees. Already furious because the governor's salary would come from the proceeds of the duty on tea, they could scarcely believe that in this way, as in so many others, Hutchinson was profiting from decisions that threatened their own liberties. There was, moreover, the question of principle. As many saw it, North's legislation was designed to encourage—some said bribe— the colonists to purchase East India tea and pay the duty, hence implicitly admitting that Parliament had the right to tax the colonies. From his vantage point in London, Franklin urged Americans to stand firm, convinced that if they continued their boycott, Parliament would have to bow to necessity and abolish the tax on tea.[23]

Franklin's advice was unnecessary. Even those colonists who had ignored the boycott in the past now seemed determined to avoid buying Company tea, convinced that to do otherwise would signal their willingness to be taxed by Parliament. As talk of resistance spread, the Sons of Liberty swung into action, vowing to make sure that no East India tea would be unloaded on American shores and no one would pay the hated tax. In many port cities, the Sons were successful. Consignees in New York and Philadelphia reluctantly announced that they would not attempt to sell any dutied tea, and everyone assumed that ships carrying the unwanted cargo would be turned back before their crews even attempted to unload it. In Boston, however, the arrival of the tea in the city's harbor precipitated a showdown not only between England and Massachusetts but also between the leaders of the anti-tax movement and Thomas Hutchinson.

As chief justice of Massachusetts, as lieutenant governor of the colony, and finally as governor, Hutchinson had routinely insisted on enforcing obedience to Parliament's efforts to tax the colonies, even though he conceded that those efforts were unwise, if not unconstitutional. He was more than willing to concede that Parliament shouldn't tax its colonies. Beyond that, he would not go. While he had repeatedly begged London officials to repeal the duty on tea, he would never countenance overt disobedience to the law. His sense of honor, and the oath he had sworn when he assumed office, told him that he had no other choice. Thus, Hutchinson vowed that whenever East India tea arrived in Boston, the cargo would be unloaded and the tax paid. This would be one time when Massachusetts would be noted for its obedience to Parliament instead of as the leader of colonial protests.

Bostonians were prepared when the ship *Dartmouth* sailed into Boston Harbor on November 28, 1773. Their popular leaders had already exerted strong, ultimately futile pressure on the tea consignees, harassing them and even making not-so-veiled threats to spill blood if the malefactors refused to resign their positions. In official town meetings as well as in extralegal committees they resolved not to buy any East India tea. Thus, as soon as the *Dartmouth* arrived, Boston leaders paid a visit to Francis Rotch, the son of the ship's owner, demanding that he return to England immediately taking his tea with him. Even if Rotch wanted to comply with this instruction, his hands were tied. Neither the *Dartmouth* nor two other tea-bearing ships that arrived later could legally depart for home without unloading and paying duties on their cargo. And by law, twenty days after the ships dropped anchor, duties on all taxable goods aboard the vessels had to be collected. If the taxes were not paid, Hutchinson could order customs officials to board the ships, unload their cargo, and store it in warehouses until the crisis was over. Then Hutchinson could quietly turn the confiscated goods over to the consignees. It was possible, even likely, that many "patriotic" Bostonians would buy the tea, tempted by the lower prices. Thus the tax would surely be paid. No matter how much they may have wanted to leave Massachusetts, Rotch and the other captains were stuck in Boston Harbor. Hutchinson ordered vessels from the British navy to block the tea ships' departure. A makeshift militia under the command of merchant John Hancock refused to let the captains unload the tea.

Boston leaders kept up the pressure. Organizers spread out, securing the support of other Massachusetts towns for their endeavors. They also continued to beg Hutchinson to let the ships depart, thus making a confrontation unnecessary. But the governor ignored their pleas. Instead, he left Boston for his country home in Milton, planning to ride out the storm. Thoroughly frustrated, radical leaders made their next move. At the end of November, they invited everyone to an unofficial (Governor Hutchinson called it illegal) town meeting at Faneuil Hall, Boston's public marketplace, to decide what to do next. The building was not nearly big enough for the throngs, many from outside Boston, who showed up. Thus they moved to the Old South Meeting House, where over 6,000 people—easily the biggest crowd in any colony in a decade—gathered. There they resolved once more that the tea should be returned to England, but to no avail. The consignees had fled to the safety of Castle William and they resolutely refused to resign their positions.

On the afternoon of December 14, just three days before Governor Hutchinson could legally confiscate the tea, a crowd gathered once more at the Old South Church. They ordered Rotch to seek permission from the customs commissioner to leave the harbor. Presented with a resolute escort of ten men, Rotch reluctantly obeyed, but the commissioner turned down his request. The stage was set for a showdown.

Two days later, 5,000 inhabitants gathered yet again at the Old South Church. Still searching for a peaceful end to the crisis, Boston leaders instructed Rotch to appeal directly to Governor Hutchinson. Rotch complied, but when he returned from Milton three hours later, the news was grim. Hutchinson had rejected his request. As men like Samuel Adams saw it, no desirable option remained. If Bostonians destroyed the tea they would invite the retribution of England. The city might well be subject to martial law, and ringleaders would no doubt be branded as rebels. Yet to allow the tea to be unloaded was unthinkable. They had made every conceivable effort to avoid this moment. But Hutchinson and his minions in the Customs Office would not allow them so much as a face-saving gesture. Thus, a plan that had probably been in the works for weeks went into operation. Disguised as Indians, a group of men silently boarded the vessels, split all 340 chests of tea with their axes, and threw the entire cargo into the ocean. The participants in the Boston Tea Party, most of whose names remain as shrouded in secrecy today as they were in 1773, had directly challenged Parliament's right to tax the colonies and the government's ability to protect the property of innocent Englishmen.

Benjamin Franklin blamed Lord North and even more Thomas Hutchinson for the destruction of the tea. Still, the man Wedderburn characterized as the "great incendiary" was shocked by the events of December 16. He could not imagine how the situation had gotten out of hand so quickly. He had been a consistent and vociferous proponent of the nonimportation movement. Economic pressure, he insisted, was legal and, more importantly, it would inevitably lead to a change in Parliament's policy. Was there really, he wondered, a "Necessity for carrying Matters to such Extremity, as in a Dispute about

Publick Rights, to destroy private Property"? He immediately urged Boston leaders to offer to "repair the Damage and make Compensation to the Company."[24] Such a gesture just might, he thought, "remove much of the Prejudice now entertain'd against us," giving Massachusetts at least some chance to deflect the anger directed at the colony from all directions.[25]

Franklin was fully aware of just how angry London officials were. The colonists had never had so few friends in the capital city. The "violent Destruction of the Tea," he reported, "seems to have united all Parties" against Massachusetts.[26] Members of the administration were already interrogating colonists newly arrived in London who might tell them more about what had transpired in Boston and, more to the point, who was to blame. Legal experts had given their opinion that the destruction of the tea was high treason, for which the punishment was death. Throughout London, voices could be heard demanding draconian measures to punish not just a few rabbel rousers but all of Massachusetts for the actions of a "wrong-headed mob."[27] While Franklin still wanted to spare the Bay Colony the consequences of its ill-conceived actions, after his appearance at the Cockpit he knew that he had no leverage to do so.

The Boston Tea Party and the quarrel over independent salaries for Crown officials provided the context for Franklin's appearance at the Cockpit. But Franklin had to have known that he himself bore considerable responsibility for Alexander Wedderburn's highly personal and undeniably vicious attacks on January 29. For even as the futile constitutional debate between Hutchinson and his assembly was drawing to its inconclusive end, and long before the Tea Party had occurred, Benjamin Franklin was, however unintentionally, setting in motion a process that led to his own humiliation and also destroyed whatever remained of Hutchinson's ability to resolve his differences with Massachusetts.

The groundwork for the debacle at the Cockpit had been laid years earlier. Between 1768 and 1769 Thomas Hutchinson had written occasional letters to Thomas Whately, a Member of Parliament, a former secretary of the treasury, and one of the staunchest supporters of George Grenville, chief minister from 1763 to 1765. At about the same time, Andrew Oliver, Hutchinson's brother-in-law, was also corresponding with Whately. Oliver was then a member of the Massachusetts Council, the upper house of the legislature that also served as an advisory board for the governor. Both Oliver and Hutchinson had been victims of mob violence in 1765 because most people in the colony believed that they supported the Stamp Act, one of Parliament's earliest efforts to tax its mainland possessions. Oliver was less restrained in his condemnation of colonial democracy run amok than Hutchinson, but both men were clearly worried. They painted the actions of the Stamp Act rioters in lurid detail and advocated a firm policy to shore up the power of royal government in Massachusetts. Hutchinson, in particular, feared that colonial resistance would lead England to overreact, hence resulting in the loss of the very liberties that Massachusetts malcontents claimed they wanted to protect. Parliament, he thought, must establish its control over the colonies before it was too late. Otherwise, an attempt at independence—which to his mind meant complete chaos—would be the inevitable result.

Both the Hutchinson letters and the Oliver letters were private—although in the eighteenth century, the notion of privacy was surely a loose one. Somewhat ironically, Benjamin Franklin had always vociferously complained when he suspected—with good reason—that his own private letters were being intercepted by London officials. Indeed, because Hutchinson knew how difficult it was to maintain any sort of confidentiality whenever he put pen to paper, he regularly directed his correspondents not to divulge the contents of his missives. Nevertheless, Whately had shared all or parts of the letters with many disgruntled Englishmen, and Hutchinson's correspondence had floated around London with considerable ease. When Francis Bernard, governor of Massachusetts during the Stamp Act crisis, arrived in London after having been relieved of his post, he had used snippets of Hutchinson's letters to show the Bay Colony in the worst possible light. Ignoring those passages that urged London to exercise caution and to avoid military force, Bernard and other Englishmen who were critical of what they saw as lenience toward the colonies highlighted Hutchinson's opinion that fundamental changes in the Massachusetts government were essential if independence was to be avoided. While it is doubtful that Hutchinson knew how Bernard, Grenville, and others were using his letters, he grew ever more cautious and secretive, especially after 1770, thus fueling the very suspicions he was trying to dispel. He lived in fear that despite his elaborate precautions, his enemies would get hold of his correspondence, twist his words, and quote him out of context, thus "proving" that he was an enemy to the people of Massachusetts. In 1772, those fears became a reality.

Thomas Whately died in 1772, but the letters that Hutchinson and Oliver sent him survived. Grenville had lent those missives "to another" and when he died before their borrower returned them, someone—Franklin resolutely refused to divulge his informant's identity to anyone, and historians still do not know who he was—gained possession of the letters and handed them over to Benjamin Franklin.[28] At the beginning of December 1772 Franklin wrote to Thomas Cushing, the Massachusetts Speaker of the House. "There has," he said with studied casualness, "lately fallen into my Hands Part of a Correspondence that I have reason to believe laid the Foundation of most if not all our present Grievances." When Franklin sent the letters to the Speaker, he urged Cushing neither to copy nor to publish them and to show them only to those "men of Worth in the Province" whose discretion he could trust.[29]

Franklin's explanation for his decision to share the Hutchinson/ Oliver letters with Cushing seems naïve, at least in hindsight. He claimed that when he saw what the two Massachusetts leaders had written, he was immediately convinced that he understood why the king and Parliament were so inexplicably eager to destroy colonial liberties. Now, at least for Franklin, everything was clear. "Those Measures were projected, advised and called for by Men of Character among ourselves," he said. Hutchinson and Oliver had intentionally done all they could to "mislead" London officials, hence moving the government to enact a series of "arbitrary Measures" that it would never have embraced under any other circumstances. As a result, Franklin concluded triumphantly, "my own Resentment [of parliamentary policy] has by this means been considerably abated." And he hoped that when Cushing and his cohorts read the letters, their reaction would echo his own. As he explained the matter to his longtime friend—and future loyalist—Pennsylvanian Joseph Galloway, he believed the letters "would remove much of their Resentment against Britain as a harsh unkind Mother, lay the Blame where it ought to lay, and by that means promote a Reconciliation."[30]

As for Hutchinson and Oliver themselves, Franklin had nothing but contempt. "When," he fulminated, "I find them bartering away the Liberties of their native Country for Posts, and negociating for Salaries and Pensions, for which the Money is to be squeezed from the People . . . calling for Troops to protect and secure the Enjoyment of them; when I see them exciting Jealousies in the Crown, and provoking it to Wrath against a great Part of its faithful Subjects; creating Enmities between the different Countries of which the Empire consists," there was no room for doubt. The two men were "Betrayers of the Interest, not of their Native Country only, but of the Government they pretend to serve, and of the whole English Empire."[31] Franklin thought the letters let the king and Parliament off the hook. The explanation for all the quarrels dividing Parliament and the colonies lay with Thomas Hutchinson and Andrew Oliver. A couple of selfish and ambitious Americans were to blame for everything.

Franklin never retreated from his claim that he sent the letters to Massachusetts in an "endeavour to lessen the breach between two states of the same empire," nor did he ever stop blaming England for failing to take advantage of the golden opportunity he had provided.[32] Had the ministry been "disposed to a Reconciliation, as they sometimes pretend to be," he complained, then it could have pointed to the letters to explain its previous errors in judgment. Instead, "this Opportunity our Ministers had not the Wisdom to embrace."[33]

When the letters reached Boston in March 1773, Hutchinson's debate with the assembly over the nature of the British constitution had just reached its painful and inconclusive end. Cushing made a half-hearted effort to comply with Franklin's instructions, sharing the missives with a handful of men. But news of the explosive documents soon leaked out, and the pressure to publish them was intense. As wild rumors spread, even Andrew Oliver began to argue that everyone should see what he actually wrote, assuming that the truth was much less damaging than the accounts that were raging throughout the entire colony and beyond. On June 15, Cushing agreed to publish the letters. Immediately, the assembly drew up a set of resolutions berating Hutchinson and Oliver, maintaining that the two men had intentionally tried to subvert the liberties of the people of Massachusetts. The lawmakers went so far as to blame both men for the heinous Boston Massacre. Under the circumstances, they argued that they had no choice but to beg the king to remove the governor and lieutenant governor from their offices. Both Hutchinson and Oliver had irrevocably lost the confidence of the colony, and hence their continuance in power served no practical purpose. It was an audacious demand—both men served at the discretion of the Crown, not the colonists. Still, Franklin dutifully presented the petition to Lord Dartmouth, secretary of state for the American Department.[34] It was this petition that served as the occasion for Franklin's appearance at the Cockpit.

Hutchinson was devastated by the response to the publication of his letters. He was already unpopular; the letters simply made matters worse. Vilified at home and in the Bay Colony and beyond, burned in effigy, the object of anger and ridicule everywhere, he did not know where to turn or how to respond. To be accused of being the prime mover in a plot to destroy the liberties of his native Massachusetts, a colony he viewed with complete devotion, was simply unthinkable. Hutchinson, who—like Benjamin Franklin, ironically enough—loved both Empire and colony, who had done all he could to bring England and America closer together, had to concede defeat. His only recourse was to do what he could to salvage his own name. Thus at the end of June he asked Dartmouth for a leave of absence so that he could travel to London, talk to Members of Parliament in person, explain his actions, and perhaps secure the exoneration from the home government that eluded him in the country of his birth. Only the colony's reaction to the Tea Act made him delay his departure.

In the beginning, very few people—not including his own son— knew that Franklin had been responsible for sending the Hutchinson and Oliver letters to Thomas Cushing. But in December 1773 Thomas Whately's brother William challenged former customs official John Temple to a duel, convinced that Temple had given Franklin the letters. Temple had always blamed Hutchinson for the loss of his lucrative post in Massachusetts, and thus he was not an unlikely culprit. Neither man was seriously injured in the contretemps, but less than a month before his appearance at the Cockpit, Franklin, hoping to prevent "further mischief," announced publicly that he "alone" had "obtained and transmitted to Boston the letters in question."[35]

All of London was abuzz, transfixed by Franklin's admission. The usual "courtiers," Franklin acknowledged, were "highly enraged" and the press was "filled with invectives" against him. There were even rumors that he would soon be incarcerated in Newgate Prison.[36] His enemies thought Franklin's perfidy was to be expected. An anonymous letter in London's *Morning Post* asserted that the American agent's "rectitude and honesty" had always been "very much doubted." Now those doubts were stronger than ever. London's *Public Advertiser* went even further, asserting that Franklin was "one of the most determined enemies of the welfare and prosperity of Great Britain."[37] And to make matters worse, Lord Dartmouth selected this moment to present the Massachusetts petition for the removal of Hutchinson and Oliver to the king. Official London put two and two together and came to the conclusion that it was Benjamin Franklin's fault that the relationship between colony and country had disintegrated to so sorry a state.

Thus no one was surprised when Alexander Wedderburn's Cockpit oration focused on Franklin's role in publicizing the Hutchinson/Oliver letters. It was Franklin, after all, who "surreptitiously obtained" the private correspondence of a private individual and who thus had stirred up "groundless, Vexatious and Scandalous" complaints against Hutchinson and Oliver.[38] Wedderburn would have opposed the Massachusetts petition in any case, and the Boston Tea Party would have given him an excuse to use the most vitriolic language. But the Hutchinson/Oliver letters led him to target Benjamin Franklin as well. By his own actions, Franklin had given government officials someone to blame for all their anger and frustration. They were looking for a scapegoat, and Franklin, not Hutchinson or Oliver, fit the bill.

Wedderburn took each of Franklin's explanations for having sent the Whately correspondence to Boston and, to the satisfaction of most members of the audience, demolished each of them. It was, of course, ludicrous to imagine that exposure of the letters would lead to a reconciliation between Crown and colony. To the contrary, the letters gave Massachusetts lawmakers their rationale as they sought to persuade the king to remove Hutchinson from office. Franklin's actions, therefore, were not only morally reprehensible but also appeared to be responsible for the radicalization of Massachusetts. If his motives were so pure, asked Wedderburn, then why did he try to keep his part in the affair a secret? Moreover, if, as Franklin insisted, he had simply done his duty as a colonial agent who was obliged to give his constituents all the pertinent information at his disposal, then why did he fail to send the letters to the entire assembly? Why did he restrict access to the letters to a few select men—all of whom were clearly members of his conspiratorial junto? Was it not obvious that he was trying to manipulate the "innocent well-meaning farmers, which compose the bulk of the Assembly," leading them to believe the worst about two men who had served them so well?[39]

Most members of the Privy Council left the Cockpit on January 29 convinced that they had won a major victory against Benjamin Franklin and those he represented. Moreover, they were determined to capitalize on that victory. Still smarting from the news of the Tea Party, they were more resolute than ever. They were bent on acting before it was too late, securing the respect of the other colonies, and forcing Massachusetts to repudiate the radicals who operated so freely within its borders. England would no longer back down from its insistence that the colonies recognize parliamentary sovereignty. It would enforce the law and collect its taxes, and it would mete out the harshest possible punishments it could devise to all of Massachusetts until Bostonians had paid for the tea its rabble rousers had so cavalierly destroyed.

Neither Franklin nor Hutchinson was so triumphant. The governor was gratified as the accounts of Franklin's humiliation drifted across the Atlantic. Still, the entire affair had been excruciatingly painful. It had changed his life—and not for the better—forever. No matter how low Franklin's reputation had sunk in London, Hutchinson's position in Massachusetts did not improve. Thus, the governor continued to make plans to leave home for what he hoped would be a temporary exile. He finally left his Milton retreat on June 1, 1774 and reached London a month later. Lord Dartmouth contacted him almost as soon as he arrived. The two men talked for over an hour before the secretary convinced him—although he was hardly dressed for the occasion—to go immediately to Court to meet with George III. How comforting it must have been to hear the king assure him that "nothing could be more cruel than the treatment you met with in betraying your private letters."[40] And in the days that followed, the governor was besieged by the city's notables, all of whom valued his thoughts on colonial affairs and eagerly offered him their "strongest professions of affection and esteem."[41]

Despite all the wining and dining he enjoyed when he first arrived in England, Hutchinson was not content. He was almost obsessed by his determination to find out who had given his letters to Benjamin Franklin. His new London friends were as fascinated by the topic as he was. A great number, including William Whately, claimed to have it on good authority that, despite Franklin's claims to the contrary, John Temple was indeed the culprit.[42] But on August 8, Temple himself made a surprise visit to Hutchinson. He was determined to forget all of their old differences and to assure the governor that he had no part in the affair of the letters, nor did he have any idea how Franklin had managed to get them. Portraying himself as a victim of malignant gossips, he protested that the duel that he had fought with Whately was one of the most "devastating" experiences he had ever endured.[43]

Although he did not quit trying, Hutchinson never got to the bottom of the matter. The "affair," he said at the end of the summer, is "still in a strange state." Temple's protestations of innocence appeared to be genuine. Indeed, Hutchinson told Dartmouth, if he was lying, he was "a most dangerous man." But if not Temple, who?[44] Both Dartmouth and Whately continued to insist that Hutchinson need look no further than John Temple. There were, said Whately darkly, "circumstances enough to put it out of doubt that he took them."[45] But by January, even Whately—who was at least as consumed by the entire business as Hutchinson was—had backtracked. He now had evidence, he said, that "exculpates Temple" entirely.[46]

While Hutchinson went to his grave not knowing the answer to a question that never stopped haunting him, one thing seemed absolutely clear to the governor and virtually all of his London friends. Benjamin Franklin's decision to send the Hutchinson/Oliver letters to Massachusetts was the direct antecedent of the final breach between England and America. "What has that man to answer for?" asked one of the governor's acquaintances. "If it had not been for that most wicked proceeding about your letters, England and the Colonies would now have been reconciled."[47] Significantly, there were some—but never Hutchinson—who actually thought this was all to the good. In particular, Lord Hillsborough, former head of the Board of Trade as well as the first secretary of state for the American Department, insisted that Parliament would still have been dallying to no discernable effect had it not been for Benjamin Franklin's acknowledgment that he was responsible for sending Hutchinson's letters to Boston. Now, he smiled, the government was virtually forced to act.[48]

Hutchinson may have been pleased with the support he received from nearly every corner, but he was miserable in most other respects. While few in the colonies would ever believe it, the governor strove mightily to persuade members of the Privy Council, and even the king himself, to modify their harsh stance. Hutchinson thought the Coercive Acts of 1774 were much too draconian. He was unhappy because they severely curtailed the autonomy of local government in Massachusetts and prepared the way for General Thomas Gage to run the colony by martial law. As a former merchant whose sons still made a living in trans-Atlantic commerce, he vehemently opposed the provision that closed the Port of Boston until the colony had paid for the tea that a handful of men had destroyed.[49] And he was dispirited when he realized that both the king and Parliament had ignored his warnings that their legislation would, if anything, be counterproductive. Parliament, he confided to his son, had "gone too far here to recede, let the opposition in America be what it will."[50] He would have been unhappier still had he known that the king, no doubt deliberately, had misrepresented his views to Lord North. Hutchinson, said the king, thought the Government's bill was well calculated to get the people of Massachusetts to submit.[51]

Hutchinson always wanted the best for Massachusetts, and he longed for the time when colony and country would be reconciled. Unlike most royal governors, he was an American whose very identity was tied to the place of his birth. His diary entries were peppered with affectionate references to the only home that he had ever known. "My thoughts," he would say, "day and night are upon New England."[52] When he returned to London after a trip to the opulent city of Bath, he insisted that his pleasures there did not compare to the joys of home. "Indeed," he wrote to his son, "I had rather live in obscurity there than in pomp and splendor here."[53] He found it impossible to "subdue a natural attachment to the very soil and air, as well as to the people of New England." Above all, he longed, he said, to "lay my bones in my native soil."[54]

Franklin, too, was devastated not only by his ordeal at the Cockpit but also by its immediate aftermath. His reputation was in shreds, and his usefulness to the colonies was at an end. Thus, one of Hutchinson's few satisfactions was his knowledge that Benjamin Franklin was suffering more than he was. Indeed, the governor was almost as focused on tracking Franklin's every move as he was in finding out who had given the Massachusetts agent his letters. Almost as soon as he arrived in London, Hutchinson inquired about Franklin's whereabouts. Lord Dartmouth had it on the best authority that Franklin—whom he, like Wedderburn, had begun calling the "great Incendiary"—was leaving for America but had not yet departed.[55] By the end of August, the governor had still not set eyes on his nemesis. His sources assured him that this was because Franklin was afraid to show his face in public. He had not, they said, appeared "in any company he used to frequent since his business with Whatley."[56] They insisted that he was not even welcome at either the Royal Society or the Philosophical Society.[57] Occasionally Franklin brought a petition to Dartmouth's attention, but outside of that, he remained well out of sight. Hutchinson gleefully noted every sign of the disapprobation with which his fellow American was held, and he smiled whenever someone told him of any slight, no matter how trivial, that Franklin endured.[58] Hutchinson believed that the Massachusetts agent "never recovered his credit to the least degree." He had heard that even Franklin's own son William, the royal governor of New Jersey, had condemned his father's actions. Admittedly, the governor suspected that William was acting upon Benjamin's orders, as a ploy to keep his own sinecure intact. But it was just possible that everyone—even his nearest and dearest relations—had deserted their erstwhile hero.[59]

If Hutchinson exaggerated Benjamin Franklin's discomfort, it was not by much. Franklin insisted that in the days following the Privy Council's hearing he was visited by countless well-wishers who expressed their "Indignation at the unworthy Treatment he received." He claimed not to have lost a single friend as a result of the incident.[60] Be that as it may, even some of his admirers were hard put to defend Franklin's decision to use private letters for public purposes. And it became obvious that the ministry (the amorphous and fluid administrative and bureaucratic arm of the Crown) was determined to punish him for his sins. Two days after his appearance at the Cockpit, Franklin was dismissed from his position as the king's deputy postmaster of the American colonies. Although he was furious at yet another blow to his pride, he tried to make the best of his fall from grace. He maintained that he had no need of the money his position had provided him. And he was happy that "no Failure of Duty in my Office is alleg'd against me." He had served long and well, he said, and under his "good management," the postal system had thrived. In the end, he claimed to be proud of his dismissal. As he told his sister, Jane Mecom, "intending to disgrace me, they have rather done me Honour." He had been fired because of his "great Offence" in sending the Hutchinson/Oliver letters to Boston, and because he was simply "too much attach'd to the Interests of America." Thus the loss was a "Testimony of my being uncorrupted."[61] But if Franklin and his supporters saw him as a martyr, his enemies thought he had gotten his just deserts.

More painful by far was the rift that the affair of the letters had exposed between Benjamin and his son William. Hutchinson was on the right track when he mentioned William's unhappiness with his father's part in the business. But he was wrong to suspect that the rumored rupture between the two Franklins was fabricated. William never forgave Benjamin for sending Governor Hutchinson's letters to the Massachusetts Assembly, and Benjamin was hurt when William did not offer him so much as a word of sympathy once he learned of his treatment at the hands of Alexander Wedderburn. What both men had begun to sense even before January 1774—that their opinions had begun to diverge markedly—was made abundantly clear after Benjamin's humiliation at the Cockpit. They could no longer ignore their differences. Their once-close personal and political relationship was about to come to an end, and there was little that either man could do about it.

So long as he remained in London, Franklin did what he could to serve the colonies. That his influence had rapidly diminished went without saying. He immediately resigned his position as Massachusetts agent, although he continued to promote the colony's interests unofficially. He wrote an account of his experience at the Cockpit, having it printed in various venues throughout Massachusetts, thus making sure that everyone at home would hear the "accurate" version of his treatment. Still, he continued to publish his thoughts on the state of Anglo-American relations in London's newspapers, putting colonial actions in the most positive light. And even as he was predicting that war was inevitable, he was still looking for a way to reconcile those who insisted upon quarrelling over "a paltry threepenny Duty on Tea."[62]

Although Franklin remained in London for over a year after his appearance at the Cockpit, using his time in a futile attempt to hold the Empire together, it became increasingly clear that no one—including Franklin—was willing to back down. As he dealt with various well-placed Englishmen who were trying to negotiate some sort of compromise, Franklin was increasingly obdurate, standing on principle, drawing ever firmer lines in the sand. Once Parliament insisted upon explicit colonial recognition of its absolute sovereignty, he knew that an honorable accommodation was impossible.

In the end, Franklin sailed for home empty-handed, leaving London before the affair of the letters destroyed him altogether. Indeed, it was further fallout from the debacle that probably led him to depart when he did. Almost immediately after the Privy Council had rendered its decision on the Massachusetts petition, William Whately—for whom Franklin had done many favors over the years—filed a suit against him in Chancery Court. The suit included a long catalog of accusations, most of which were palpably untrue. Among other things, it said that Franklin had made numerous copies of the letters and intended to sell them—for a profit. And of course Whately demanded that Franklin divulge the name of the person who had given him the letters.[63] Franklin was convinced that Whately was not acting on his own. He was fully aware that his own enemies were using Whately to harass him. This, from Franklin's perspective, gave a "still meaner" aspect to the entire business.[64] Franklin fought a delaying action against Whately's suit as long as possible, steadfastly refusing to divulge the name of his informant. But in the end, he managed to escape judgment—and perhaps jail—by fleeing the country altogether.[65]

It is impossible to overstate the significance of this ordeal to Benjamin Franklin. It was both a personally and a politically devastating moment. It is surely no accident that, on the very day that he signed the Franco-American Treaty of Alliance in 1778, he donned the same suit of Manchester velvet he wore at the Cockpit. Franklin insisted that he immediately put the entire incident out of his mind; he did nothing to try to get back at his persecutors, and he did not even make an effort to justify his part in the debacle. He "held a cool sullen Silence," he said, "reserving my self to some future Opportunity."[66] That was not exactly true. Before he left England for good, Franklin began to compose another document in his own defense. Never published—never even completed—it revealed a man angry and unforgiving about his public humiliation. Franklin reiterated his reasons for sending the letters to Massachusetts, and he rejected the insinuations of those who thought that exposing private letters to the light of day was by definition dishonorable. He pointed out that the ministry had on many occasions intercepted his own "private" letters and had used them for its own wicked purposes. Yet the very people who attacked his behavior did not seem to think that the ministry's actions were especially unacceptable or even unusual.

But what rankled most were the accusations that he was an "incendiary." He, whose love for the Empire was surpassed by no man's, who had done all he could to minimize the differences between England and its colonies, was now vilified as the person whose actions had single-handedly destroyed any chance of peace. If that was what his enemies thought, so be it.

No matter how much Franklin clung to his image as an amicable man who saw all sides of any issue and who was always willing to split the difference in the interests of peace, it is nevertheless true that he was no stranger to controversy. He was a political animal, who had been involved in more than his share of public quarrels, and he generally gave as good as he got. That being the case, why was this particular event so excruciating for him? In part, of course, Franklin simply saw his treatment as the last in a long series of affronts to colonial dignity that he had witnessed over the years. To him, it was evidence that England was not interested in accommodation and that the ministry had no desire to preserve colonial liberties.

But there was more to it than that. This was personal. And it was personal in large part because of Franklin's own life story. Benjamin Franklin was a self-made man whose formative years had been lived in a part of the Empire where status was coveted but never certain and not always even recognizable. Especially in colonial cities, where strangers rubbed shoulders with one another almost daily, and where people had to size one another up as quickly and accurately as possible, appearances and reputation mattered. Indeed, in a fluid society where few people really knew their place, reputation was everyone's most valuable possession. Thus, from the time he had fled stuffy and hidebound Boston for the new and more open city of Philadelphia, Franklin had been aware of the need to present himself in the most positive light. His own *Autobiography* is replete with examples of his obsession with creating and preserving his image. He never forgot that Deborah Read, his future wife, had laughed at him on the day he arrived in his new home because of the ridiculous figure he cut as he walked down Market Street with three large "puffy rolls" under his arms.[67] A few years later, he vowed to quit working for printer Samuel Keimer because his boss berated him in front of the other workers. Keimer's "loud Voice," Franklin admitted, "nettled me the more for their Publicity, all the Neighbors who were looking out on the same Occasion being Witnesses how I was treated."[68] That sort of humiliation could not be tolerated by a man who knew that he was, in essence, what he appeared to be and what people thought that he was. To lose face was to lose not only respectability but power. It was to make it virtually impossible for him to be successful in business or to exert his influence on public affairs. Once Franklin endured Alexander Wedderburn's wrath, his usefulness in London was over. And he knew it. He had entered the Cockpit as a loyal Englishman. He left it as an American patriot.

....

CHAPTER 2

Present at the Cockpit

Almost everyone who was anyone in England's power elite crowded into the Cockpit on January 29. Many of those present were—or would be—major players in the drama that pitted the colonists against England in the last quarter of the eighteenth century. The luminaries in attendance ranged from Franklin's most virulent enemies to relatively sympathetic acquaintances. Four were especially knowledgeable about and interested in colonial affairs. All had met Franklin; some knew him personally. None was a disinterested observer. Wills Hill, Lord Hillsborough, not only was a major irritant to most colonists but was Franklin's personal nemesis as well. Frederick, Lord North, was already the king's chief minister, a position he would retain until after the defeat of Lord Cornwallis at Yorktown in 1781. General Thomas Gage's presence was fortuitous. He happened to be in England only briefly, checking in with his superiors and enjoying a well-deserved respite from his responsibilities as commander in chief of His Majesty's North American forces. He would shortly be dispatched to Boston to head a military government aimed at regaining control of Massachusetts in the wake of the Tea Party. Edmund Burke, one of the few Members of Parliament who—to a degree—sympathized with the colonies, was also there. He came away more convinced than ever that American—and perhaps more to the point, British—liberties were in jeopardy.

The English government in the eighteenth century was not a vast and faceless bureaucracy. All of those present at the Cockpit not only knew one another but lived in a world where personal connections mattered. Often as not, London politicians gained favor or fell from grace as the result of who their friends and relatives were and how they got along. Benjamin Franklin had lived in the English capital for a decade. When he stood before the Privy Council and stared at the raucous spectators, he was looking at people he knew. These were men with whom he did business. He had fought with some, and shared a joke, a smile, or a glass of Madeira or claret with others. He had admired many of them, and at one time he had aspired—he thought with good reason—to be one of their number. To be laughed at by these men was to be rejected in a very personal and painful way.

Some, Lord Hillsborough and General Gage, in particular, had axes to grind as they watched Wedderburn's performance, and their reaction to Franklin's humiliation was as emotional as it was reasoned. While Edmund Burke was the only one of the four who could muster much compassion for Benjamin Franklin, not even he truly appreciated the perspective from which most colonial leaders viewed Anglo-American relations by 1774. Ominously, all four of these men—despite their profound differences—agreed on one essential point: Parliament had the right to govern and tax the colonies. Some, particularly Burke, may have doubted the wisdom of government policy, but none questioned parliamentary supremacy. Nothing Franklin could do or say would ever alter that fundamental reality. Had he understood how united Englishmen were becoming, how few were the options open to him, Franklin would have been even less optimistic about the future of the English Empire than he was.

Lord Hillsborough was probably the most satisfied person in the Cockpit that day. As he watched Benjamin Franklin stand stoically in the face of Alexander Wedderburn's vituperative onslaught, he must have thought of it as a fitting revenge. Benjamin Franklin had helped engineer his own humiliation in this very room just two years earlier. Surely it was poetic justice that Franklin's London career would end here.

An Irish landowner of considerable means, Hillsborough had already enjoyed a long, largely successful political career. In 1763, the king made him president of the all-powerful Board of Trade which oversaw England's vast colonial empire. Five years later, he also became secretary of state of the newly created American Department. The dual appointment, which made him one of the most powerful men in England when it came to colonial affairs, seemed to make sense. Hillsborough was young—only in his forties—but he was more knowledgeable about America than many of his compatriots. True, he could be a bit stuffy and tactless, and some complained that he was much too enamored of the "Pomp and Parade of his Office."[1] Still, when Benjamin Franklin first learned of the appointment, he was not alarmed. The new secretary was surely better than former chief minister George Grenville, whose appointment would almost certainly have led to a "breach between the two countries."[2] Hillsborough had a reputation for moderation, had actually opposed the Stamp Act, and had voted for the act's repeal. He was not, Franklin assured his good friend, Joseph Galloway, "in general an enemy to America."[3]

Unfortunately, it did not take long for Franklin to begin harboring serious doubts about the secretary. Like virtually all colonists, he was taken aback by Hillsborough's aggressive defense of the king's prerogative and his unbending determination to enforce the letter of imperial law. The first sign of trouble came soon enough. As was so often the case, the quarrel originated in Massachusetts. At the beginning of 1768, the Bay Colony Assembly sent a circular letter to the lawmakers of the other mainland provinces in an effort to organize a united front opposing the recently passed Townshend Acts. As soon as he heard about this "flagitious attempt to disturb the Public Peace," Hillsborough swung into action.[4] He ordered the Massachusetts House to revoke its letter. Not surprisingly, the assembly overwhelmingly rejected Hillsborough's demand, thus forcing Governor Francis Bernard to disband the legislature. This, of course, led Boston residents to engage in ever more determined, occasionally even violent, protests against parliamentary taxation. Eventually, Hillsborough decided he had no choice but to send troops to Boston to keep the peace.

In January 1771, Hillsborough and Franklin locked horns directly. The argument, like so many that surfaced in the years before Americans declared their independence, seems relatively insignificant and overly technical to modern ears, even though it meant a great deal to many at the time. It concerned the method for appointing colonial agents. For as long as most people could remember, agents represented the interests of their entire colonies. Hence they needed the approval of governor, council, and assembly before London officials would recognize their credentials. Granted, agents representing a particular branch—usually the assembly—occasionally lobbied for a particular issue. But until 1765, that practice was the exception, not the rule. During the Stamp Act crisis, however, some agents, notably Massachusetts' Dennys De Berdt, began taking their orders from the lower house alone. Hillsborough harbored a healthy distrust of all colonial legislatures. Convinced that governors were too deferential to the popular branch, he feared that the assemblies would take advantage of this deference, throwing off what remained of their dependence on England.[5] He was determined to reverse this trend, restoring a more equitable balance between the assemblies and the governors. One way to achieve that end was to insist that agents could not represent the exclusive interests of the popular—generally most radical—branch of any colonial government.

As early as August 1768, Hillsborough had questioned De Berdt's credentials, pointing out that he was "not a regularly appointed Agent, being authorized only by the Assembly, to transact their Business."[6] Still, he tolerated the irregular appointment, judging it a fait accompli. When Franklin succeeded De Berdt, however, Hillsborough seized the opportunity to launch a determined assault on what he saw as a dangerous, even subversive practice. The Massachusetts House voted to make Franklin its representative in October 1770. Ironically, the appointment was controversial in Boston as well as in England. Many in Massachusetts distrusted Franklin, fearing that he was much too likely to seek common ground with London officialdom. Moreover, he already served three other colonies—New Jersey, Pennsylvania, and Georgia—and his son William was New Jersey's royal governor. Could he be trusted, some wondered, to devote the time and energy to serving their very needy colony? The majority decided in Franklin's favor; but from the beginning new agent was aware that there were many who preferred the more radical Arthur Lee. Perhaps because he wanted to prove his critics wrong, Franklin took an increasingly more obdurate stance toward the English government after 1770.[7]

Franklin presented his credentials to Hillsborough in January 1771. That he did so when he could easily have avoided the secretary and sought verification of his position with a potentially more sympathetic John Pownall at the Board of Trade is puzzling. If he was seeking a showdown, a chance to prove his own determination to defend colonial rights, he succeeded. Hillsborough already saw Massachusetts as his most vexing problem. And he had reason to distrust Franklin, as well. The colonial agent had recently made some rather pointed public references to the incompetence of the king's ministers, and the prickly secretary could not help but feel that at least some of those comments were aimed at him.

Franklin's account of the meeting was, of course, one-sided. The encounter, he reported, began cordially enough. Hillsborough received him almost immediately, which in itself was something of a surprise. He was used to cooling his heels for hours at a time whenever he sought an audience with government officials. But as soon as Franklin explained his business, Hillsborough's "Countenance changed." With "something between a Smile and a Sneer," the secretary indicated that he would reject Franklin's appointment. "We shall," he said, "take no Notice of any Agents but such as are appointed by Acts of Assembly to which the Governor gives his Assent." When Franklin insisted that the governor's concurrence was not necessary when it was "the Business of the People that is to be done," Hillsborough angrily disagreed. His face turning ashen, he shouted, "When I came into the Administration of American Affairs, I found them in great Disorder; By my firmness they are now something mended." If the king and his advisers do not approve of my position, he added, "they may take my Office from me when they please. I shall make 'em a Bow, and thank 'em. I shall resign with Pleasure." At that, Franklin hastily grabbed his copy of the House's appointment and stormed out of the room. But not before he fired a parting shot at the still-furious Hillsborough. "It is I believe of no great Importance whether the Appointment is acknowledged or not," he declared, "for I have not the least Conception that an Agent can at present be of any Use to any of the Colonies." He would not, he vowed, trouble his Lordship any further—on this or any other matter.[8]

Two weeks later, Franklin was still fuming. As he explained it, Hillsborough's position was an assault on colonial liberty. Moreover, the encounter led him to state publicly what he had already been thinking in private. Each colony, he wrote Speaker of the Massachusetts

House Thomas Cushing, was a separate and equal state; consequently, agents were more like "public ministers" or ambassadors for independent nations than mere lobbyists for inferior provinces. If Franklin truly believed this extraordinary conception of the Empire, he would have had a difficult time convincing anyone in England that this was the case. But he also thought that Hillsborough's position was dangerous for practical reasons. If, he insisted, an agent needed the assent of a colonial governor before the secretary would give him a seal of approval, then for all practical purposes Hillsborough would end up "appointing, or at least negativing any choice of the House of Representatives and Council," simply by instructing the governor to reject anyone with whom he was at odds. Thus, no agent who valued his job would dare to disagree with any English official, for to do so would endanger his own position.[9] Neither Hillsborough nor Franklin ever backed down. After their confrontation, the two men studiously ignored one another, and Franklin endeavored to represent Massachusetts informally even though he lacked the technical authority to do so.

The flap over agents' credentials soon blew over. Franklin's protracted quarrel with the secretary over the disposal of America's choice western lands could not be so easily resolved—and in the end it destroyed whatever small chance of amity existed between the two men. It was William Franklin, even more than his father, who had a deep and abiding love affair with the vast stretches of arable land that lay to the west of the seaboard settlements. The elder Franklin was always more at home in the city than in the countryside and could not imagine assuming the role of a gentleman farmer that seemed to fascinate his son. Still, he had never been averse to making a tidy profit in land speculation, and he was more than willing to join William and a heterogeneous group of entrepreneurs in a series of projects designed to do just that.

The obstacle in the beginning was the Proclamation of 1763. At the end of what the colonists persisted in calling the "French and Indian War," England had assumed authority over a vast amount of land, including all of Canada in the North, east and west Florida in the South, and the entire area between the Atlantic Ocean and the Mississippi River. In order to assert its control over the area as well as to avoid war between the Indians and colonists in the newly acquired territory, the Crown prohibited all private individuals from purchasing land west of the Appalachians, in effect turning the area into a vast Indian preserve. Had the Proclamation achieved its purpose, speculators would have lost out on the opportunity to buy the land cheaply and to sell it to settlers eager to escape the increasingly crowded eastern corridor.

London never managed to enforce the provisions of the Proclamation Line. There was confusion from the beginning about just where the line would be drawn, and both ordinary settlers and avaricious speculators took advantage of every uncertainty to push their own agendas. The king's ministers could do little but try to stem the tide. Especially after 1768, that thankless task fell to Lord Hillsborough. The secretary did not shrink from his duty. There were those (including Benjamin Franklin) who were convinced that as an Irish landlord, Hillsborough was opposed to any scheme that threatened to lure settlers from his own country to the American hinterland. But he had other, less self-interested motives, as well. He knew that there were many—fur traders in particular—who supported any policy that kept farmers off the land. Then, too, Hillsborough had been president of the Board of Trade during an Indian uprising known in the colonies as Pontiac's Rebellion, and as a consequence he was always reluctant to endorse a policy that threatened to stir up Indian hostilities once again. The fewer settlers there were in the West, he told General Thomas Gage, the less "Resentment of the Savages" there would be, and thus the less likelihood of another war.[10] Moreover, like many English leaders, he worried about any tendency that "might lay the foundation of a power in the heart of America."[11] The more scattered settlements became, the more difficult it would be to keep the colonies "in a just Subordination to and Dependence upon this Kingdom."[12] Finally, there was the expense such an expansion of the British domain would entail. Roads, forts, and Indian wars cost money, as did even the most rudimentary of governments. While even Hillsborough recognized that Englishmen would eventually "settle" the hinterland, he hoped to make the transition as orderly and peaceful as possible.[13]

In that final aspiration, at least, he and Franklin agreed—although their understanding of the best means to achieve that orderly end was profoundly different. Franklin knew that the Proclamation Line would not stop ordinary settlers from spilling onto the prohibited territory and putting down roots. He was convinced that allowing colonists to rush willy-nilly into the West would lead not to order but to chaos. More importantly, if "squatters" settled on the land, then it would be almost impossible for Franklin and his cohorts to profit from their own investments. No farmer who was already tilling the soil—legally or not—would be persuaded to pay a wealthy speculator for what he already considered his own. The longer the Proclamation Line remained in effect, the more farmers there would be who would simply ignore it, depriving men like Franklin of a once-in-a-lifetime opportunity to make a financial killing. Speculators from New Hampshire to Virginia had once thought the French and the Indians were the "only barrier" to their ability to profit from land sales in the West. They were distraught to discover that the government in London now stood in their way.[14]

In the spring of 1766, William sent his father a copy of the plan that he had helped to devise for the newly created Illinois Company. The project was, both Franklins thought, solid on its own merits. It was not just a land grab. It included William's pet project, the creation of a full-fledged colony in more than sixty million acres of the most fertile soil imaginable. With a respectable government in place (headed perhaps by William Franklin?), an orderly settlement would be almost guaranteed. Moreover, the French still had a great deal of influence over the natives in the Illinois country. An English colony in the region would help disrupt the Indian-French connection, thus enhancing the power and stability of the Empire. Finally, if settlers had a safe and orderly place to go, they would be much less inclined to range throughout the country, encroaching on Indian hunting grounds. Thus the likelihood of frontier warfare would be reduced. What was not to like about the plan?

The Franklins and their friends were dogged in their efforts to reap profits from the wilderness. Recognizing that connections were at least as important as solid arguments, Benjamin followed William's sage advice and offered shares in the company to "such Gentlemen of Character and Fortune in England" as he thought necessary.[15] He also contacted every official who might be willing to support his project. Some were firmly in his camp. Others could be persuaded. But the ministry, itself, was in turmoil in these years. Officeholders were appointed and fired with such dizzying speed that it was impossible to count on anyone for long. Moreover, it soon became clear that Lord Hillsborough was adamantly opposed to the entire business.

In retrospect, it seems clear that once Hillsborough assumed the presidency of the Board of Trade, the prospects for the Illinois Company were doomed. Still, the disappointing outcome did not seem so obvious at the time. "The Illinois affair goes forward," Franklin would say, "but slowly." And at times the word "slowly" seemed to represent an almost foolhardy optimism.[16]

The process was interminable. When it became clear that Hillsborough would never approve of the Illinois Company, Franklin and his cohorts formed a new company, and then another. But each met with the disapproval of the secretary. In December 1769, Franklin approached the Board of Trade yet again, asking for permission to purchase two and a half million acres of western land. He assumed with good reason that his request would meet the fate of all his previous proposals. Imagine his surprise—and his suspicion—when Hillsborough greeted his request with unprecedented magnanimity. Instead of rejecting the petition out of hand, the secretary suggested that, in fact, the request was too small! Why not, he asked, seek permission to purchase even more land—enough to create a separate colony? Although Franklin feared that Hillsborough was engaging in nothing more than a delaying tactic, he decided to take him at his word. A week later, he helped found the Grand Ohio Company, and drew up yet another proposal that was truly grandiose in its dimensions. Offering shares to as many influential Englishmen as possible— including Lord North and George Grenville—they laid plans to purchase twenty million acres of land and to create a full-fledged colony, Vandalia, in the American West.

Two years later, Franklin was still awaiting approval for a project in which he had invested more time, money, and effort than he liked to admit. Hillsborough, as Franklin had feared would be the case, proved to be adept at dragging his feet. Neither Alexander Wedderburn nor General Thomas Gage could be persuaded to support the plan. Rival speculators from Virginia also worked hard to halt the project. At one point, Franklin was sure that his dreams were about to be realized. Still, he presciently warned his son, "many things happen between the Cup and the Lip."[17]

By 1771 Franklin no longer even pretended to look for anything good to say about Lord Hillsborough. "The present American Secretary," he fulminated, is "proud, supercilious, extreamly conceited (moderate as they are) of his political Knowledge and Abilities, fond of every one that can stoop to flatter him, and inimical to all that dare tell him disagreable Truths."[18] Fortunately for Franklin, the secretary's days were numbered. In a government that at times seemed rudderless, many ambitious politicians jockeyed for power. One group in particular, known as the Bloomsbury Gang, was determined to get rid of Lord North, who had become the king's chief minister in 1770. They believed that they could unseat North by going after Hillsborough, North's most consistent supporter. Hillsborough had few friends anyway. Even the king was said to be growing tired of him. He seemed to be under fire from all sides.

In April 1772, the Board of Trade forwarded its long-awaited ruling on the Grand Ohio Company to the Privy Council. To no one's surprise, Hillsborough had used his influence to secure the Board's negative judgment. Ordinarily, the Privy Council would have rubber-stamped the Board's recommendation. Instead, a council committee stacked with company stockholders called for public hearings on the issue. On June 5, the interested parties gathered at the Cockpit. If Franklin remained silent during his appearance in the arena in 1774, in this instance he was a major player. He, along with four other shareholders, spoke forcefully in defense of the proposed grant. Less than three weeks later, the committee recommended approval of his project. Hillsborough, furious at what Edmund Burke referred to as his "Humiliation," threatened to resign unless the Privy Council rejected its own committee's recommendation and backed him up.[19] When the council called his bluff and King George refused to intercede on his behalf, he had no choice but to step down.

Ironically, the Bloomsbury Gang failed in achieving its real objective. Lord North remained in power. Only Hillsborough was gone. The dreams of the American speculators were, however, never realized—weak ministers, colonial infighting, and a growing imperial crisis all got in the way. Still, at the time it looked like a victory. Unfortunately, Hillsborough saw Franklin as largely to blame for what turned out to be just a temporary embarrassment. No wonder he was pleased as he watched Alexander Wedderburn destroy his longtime opponent in January 1774.

According to observers, Lord North's reaction to Wedderburn's performance was more circumspect than that of many who were present at the Cockpit. Nevertheless, he would not have been unhappy with what he saw. Anyone who noticed North that day—or any other—would have recognized immediately that the chief minister had not climbed to the pinnacle of parliamentary politics on the basis of his good looks. Everyone commented on his thick lips and his large bulging eyes "that rolled about to no purpose." He was fat, clumsy, and disheveled. His detractors accused him of being exceptionally lazy as well as exhibiting a marked tendency to procrastinate and to avoid responsibility. An exasperated Edmund Burke once claimed that North "blew hot and cold, and veered round the whole thirty two points of the compass of uncertainty and indecision."[20] Lord Hillsborough thought the chief minister was burdened by "too much humanity—too much religion" and thus that he was too kind to the colonists.[21] Indeed, during the crisis leading to independence, Thomas Hutchinson begged North "even with tears to resign" his position before it was too late to save the Empire.[22] Equally frustrated, though for different reasons, were those such as Burke who believed that his reluctance to take a position on any issue was evidence that North was a mere figurehead, simply doing the king's bidding without question. The more he appeared to waffle, the more convinced many were that he was simply a puppet, while George III was the puppet master pulling all the strings.[23]

Despite the complaints of naysayers, especially opposition politicians, it is fair to say that North was witty and affable, invariably self-deprecatory, and usually willing to compromise. Consequently, he seemed to get along personally with nearly everyone, even those who thought he was not quite up to the job. He had a sharp wit and was an excellent debater, the latter skill made more impressive by a loud, deep voice that drowned out all competitors for anyone's attention. Nor could even the most determined critics find so much as a hint of scandal with which to tarnish North's name.[24]

At first blush, the differences between Franklin and North appeared to be huge. Franklin was of respectable but decidedly humble birth. His ancestors were tradesmen, and his own father, Josiah, followed in the footsteps of his forebears. A silk dyer in the old country, Josiah became a candle maker in Boston. Although he did what he could to get his tenth and youngest son a decent start in life, he could hardly have imagined the heights to which Benjamin would rise. Lord

Nathaniel Dance (later Sir Nathaniel Holland), *Frederick North, 2nd Earl of Guilford*, 1773–1774. © National Portrait Gallery, London.

North, on the other hand, was born with a sense of entitlement. His family could trace its roots back to the oligarchy that had ruled England since the sixteenth century. His uncle, Lord Halifax, was president of the Board of Trade. His stepbrother was William Legge (eventually Lord Dartmouth), whose uncle, Henry Legge, had once served as Chancellor of the Exchequer. And his father, Francis North, the first Earl Guilford and the Seventh Baron North, was both wealthy and politically connected.

North enjoyed opportunities that someone like Franklin never had. After receiving the finest of educations, he embarked on the obligatory Grand Tour in 1751, dutifully polishing his already impeccable social credentials. Benjamin Franklin, to the contrary, had little formal schooling and had to wait until he was fifty-two to make his debut on the Continent. In 1754, North ran unopposed for the House of Commons, securing a seat that his father had saved especially for him. And a little over a decade later, at the age of thirty-eight, he became the First Lord of the Treasury (which in those days meant that he was the king's chief minister), a position he did not abandon until the British defeat at Yorktown.[25] Franklin, of course, never ran in any election unopposed, and he actually lost his seat in the Pennsylvania House in 1764.

Despite the obvious differences in their backgrounds and expectations, Lord North and Benjamin Franklin might have been allies— and surely would not have been enemies—in ordinary times. In fact, in 1768, when he heard that Franklin was thinking about leaving London, North offered to find the American some sort of position in the government, perhaps, ironically enough, as an undersecretary to Lord Hillsborough, if he would promise to remain in England.[26] That North would see Franklin as a potential supporter is not as surprising as it seems in retrospect. They were both essentially moderate men who often preferred to split the difference with their adversaries rather than to draw lines in the sand. They opted for humor as opposed to harsh rhetoric to win their points. And, until almost the very end, both remained loyal to King George III.

Never were the two men more on the same page than they were when they reacted to the antics of Englishman John Wilkes and his supporters in the late sixties and early seventies. An ambitious bon vivant and rabble rouser, Wilkes used his newspaper, the *North Briton*, to attack the ministry. More dangerously, he came close to libeling the king himself. In 1764, after he fled to France to avoid arrest for his inflammatory prose, he was tried and found guilty in absentia for seditious and obscene libel. Upon his return to England four years later, he began seeking a seat in the House of Commons, eventually winning election in the county of Middlesex. Parliament, however, refused to accept his credentials. Consequently, instead of serving his constituency, he ended up serving time in King's Bench Prison. He did not remain there very long, and upon his release he immediately ran for Parliament again. But each time he won a seat, Parliament—with Lord North's approval—refused to seat him. Undeterred, Wilkes won election after election, only to have the House reject his victory until 1774.

To the disgust of many, Wilkes became a popular hero, adored by crowds on both sides of the Atlantic. While he was incarcerated, a mob of some 20,000 supporters had actually marched on the prison in an effort to rescue him. When troops fired on the unarmed crowd, seven men were killed and another fifteen were injured. Shouts of "Wilkes and liberty" could be heard thereafter in both England and America. The colonists, in particular, were convinced that Wilkes's treatment proved that Parliament was trying to destroy liberty wherever it remained. And they drew obvious parallels between the deaths of Wilkes's supporters and the fate of five Bostonians who were killed during the "Boston Massacre" just two years later.

Unknown Artist, *John Wilkes*, 1769. © National Portrait Gallery, London.

Lord North, of course, deplored the attacks on persons and property in which so many of Wilkes's supporters indulged. But so did Benjamin Franklin, who characterized Wilkes as "an outlaw and exile, of bad personal character, not worth a farthing." Americans may have named both their towns and their children after John Wilkes, but Franklin—who saw firsthand the desecrated buildings, the overturned carriages, and the insults to "gentlemen and ladies of all ranks" that were the essence of the Wilkesite movement—condemned the "mischief done by drunken mad mobs to houses, windows, etc." He confided to his son, "The scenes have been horrible. London was illuminated two nights running at the command of the mob." The cost for one night's riot, he estimated, was at least 50,000 pounds.[27] Franklin had not forgotten that his own house in Philadelphia had been threatened by opponents of the Stamp Act less than three years earlier. Thus, he no doubt sympathized with North in the spring of 1771 when he heard that angry rioters had destroyed North's carriage as it headed toward the House of Commons, and that the chief minister was slightly injured in the fracas.[28]

If Lord North had looked with favor on Benjamin Franklin in the late sixties, he was not likely to do so by the time the American agent appeared at the Cockpit. His admirers always liked to characterize North as a conciliator. In reality, however, the options he considered when he addressed American affairs were few and his staunch support of parliamentary sovereignty was unwavering. He may have been willing to grant the colonies some privileges now and then, but he could never see the assemblies as equals, nor would he ever approve of American independence. In retrospect, it is easy to see that North was much less accommodating than he would admit even to himself. True enough, when he first assumed office he did not have a well-conceived program for dealing with the colonies; he seemed to have drifted into an increasingly inflexible position, and once there, he could not easily extricate himself from the mess he, himself, had helped create. Even before the Tea Party, he was determined to be "firm" with those colonists—whom he assumed were a tiny if loud minority—who were challenging Parliament's right to tax America. He had opposed the repeal of the Stamp Act in 1766, not, as he later insisted, out of loyalty to George Grenville, but because he thought that backing down would make the government look weak. In 1769, when the House of Commons received a petition from Massachusetts asking for a repeal of the Townshend Duties, North had objected even to reading the request before Parliament. Indicative of his attitude was his speech on March 5, 1770. The House was considering a repeal of the Townshend Duties. North, ever the pragmatist, supported the repeal. But when some lawmakers suggested that the tea tax should also be abandoned, he forcefully disagreed, convinced that bowing to colonial resistance would lead to even more recalcitrance in the future. Firmness, not lenience, he was convinced, was the best way to deal with stubborn Americans.

Indeed, Franklin thought that North's Tea Act was largely responsible for creating the crisis that led to the very consequence—independence—that he so vehemently deplored.[29] Admittedly, North, himself, said nothing publicly about using the act to reaffirm Parliament's right to tax the colonies. But many in America were convinced that this—not revenue, not even saving the East India Company from bankruptcy—was his "real" motive. Benjamin Franklin was one of the first to put this suspicion in writing. Parliament, he assured Thomas Cushing, was determined to "keep up the Exercise of the Right. They have no Idea that any People can act from any Principle but that of Interest; and they believe that 3d. in a Pound of Tea, of which one does not drink perhaps 10 lb in a Year, is sufficient to overcome all the Patriotism of an American!"[30] Whether or not this was indeed the chief minister's aim, North totally underestimated the colonial reaction to the Tea Act. Thus, he blundered forward, setting the stage for the hostilities that followed. If he had been determined to be unwavering before 1773, he was even more adamant after the news of Boston's destruction of the tea arrived in London less than a week before Franklin's appearance at the Cockpit. He may have been too decorous to show it, but North surely viewed Wedderburn's attacks on Benjamin Franklin with profound pleasure.

Both Lord Hillsborough and Lord North smiled upon Franklin's humiliation at the Cockpit. General Thomas Gage had no personal reason to delight in Alexander Wedderburn's vicious attacks. To the contrary, on those few occasions in the past when Gage's career had intersected directly with Franklin's, the general had been favorably impressed. Gage arrived in America in 1755 when he was posted to the colonies to serve with General Edward Braddock at the beginning of the French and Indian War. He was grateful to Franklin, whose political acumen and organizational ability helped Braddock obtain the wagons, horses, and supplies that Pennsylvania's parsimonious, Quaker-dominated government refused to provide. Despite Franklin's aid, the expedition ended in the ignominious defeat that the Pennsylvanian later described with such disdain in his *Autobiography*. Conceding that Braddock was a "brave Man," Franklin nevertheless thought the general had "too much self-confidence, too high an Opinion of the Validity of Regular Troops, and too mean a One of both Americans and Indians." Braddock's blunders, he added, with a prescience that obviously benefited from hindsight, "gave us Americans the first Suspicion that our exalted Ideas of the Prowess of British Regulars had not been well founded."[31] Whether Gage agreed with Franklin's assessment is not clear. He walked away from the battle slightly wounded, and managed to convince his superiors—in part by defending himself in the pages of Franklin's *Gazette*—that he should not be blamed for his superior's failure.

Gage's and Franklin's fortunes were intertwined again in 1764, when the Paxton Boys from western Pennsylvania marched on Philadelphia threatening to massacre those friendly Indians who had fled to the capital city in the wake of frontier violence. Franklin was part of the delegation that conducted successful negotiations with the vigilantes, persuading them to abandon their plan and return home. But he was helped in his efforts by the military reinforcements that General Gage sent to Pennsylvania. At the time, Franklin heaped fulsome praise on the army for protecting the frightened Indian refugees. Just a few years later, of course, he would not be so happy with Gage's troops.[32]

In less interesting times, Thomas Gage's career would have been viewed as successful, if undistinguished. Born somewhere in the neighborhood of 1720, he was the second son of Thomas Gage, a dissolute aristocrat, much given to gambling and drinking. Gage's mother was known primarily for her notorious promiscuity. Gage seemed determined to distance himself from his parents' unconventional behavior; consequently he was utterly undramatic and always dependable. Although like Franklin he never attended college, he was a solid and hard-working if not a dazzling student at the prestigious Westminster

School from which he graduated in 1736. Thereafter, the laws of primogeniture, which guaranteed that the first-born son would inherit a family's entire estate, dictated that he would have to make his own way in the world. Of course he had advantages and connections in this regard that Franklin most definitely lacked.

Having no land or title to inherit, Gage intelligently if not imaginatively opted for a career in the British army. It was in some ways a fortuitous choice, but in other respects it was a strange decision. Gage loved the order and discipline of army life. Like Franklin's son William, he was comfortable in a world that respected hierarchy and where everyone knew his place. Still, having witnessed the sights and sounds of the battlefield on more than one occasion, he knew what armchair generals did not. The blood and gore of actual warfare was something to be avoided at almost any cost.

Despite his mediocre performance on the battlefield, he was suited to military life and he climbed steadily in the ranks. His brother's influence, his own ability to purchase appointments, and his uncanny tendency to be in the right place at the right time meant that his fortunes continued to rise. He remained in America at the end of the French and Indian War, taking advantage of the government's dissatisfaction with General Jeffrey Amherst to become the Commander of His Majesty's forces in North America in 1763.[33]

Thomas Gage was comfortable in his role as peacetime general. He enjoyed the support of George III, who admired his self-discipline and praised his efforts to keep his expenditures to an absolute minimum. He may not have been much of a military tactician, but he was a gifted bureaucrat who generally managed to avoid controversy, in large part by telling his superiors what they wanted to hear. Gage not only liked his job, he approved of much of what he encountered in America. He quickly put down roots in what he began to see as his adopted home. He married wealthy Margaret Kemble of New Jersey, and over the years bought extensive tracts of land in New York, Canada, and Montserrat. Cautious and generally fair-minded, like North—and Franklin—he always characterized himself as a moderate. If he took the sovereignty of King-in-Parliament for granted, he was also a determined defender of British liberties. And although he was a stern commander, he was seldom arbitrary. He was certainly not a tyrant.

Nevertheless, no matter how fair and judicious he may have seemed to many observers, Gage was destined to frustrate Benjamin Franklin in some important respects. Most obvious early on, he agreed with Hillsborough's opposition to Franklin's speculation in western land. Even before Hillsborough became secretary of state for the American Department, astute observers suspected that Gage had "imbibed unfavourable and very unjust Sentiments" concerning the Franklins' plans.[34] Fearful of an Indian uprising that might be even more devastating than Pontiac's Rebellion, determined to administer England's mainland possessions as cheaply as possible, Gage was particularly hostile to the "schemes" of those who dreamed of founding new colonies in the interior.[35] Even after Hillsborough's forced retirement in 1772, Gage worked tirelessly—and successfully—behind the scenes to defeat Benjamin Franklin's project.[36]

Gage's perspective on the nature of the Empire was also bound to set him at odds with the colonists in general, and Benjamin Franklin in particular. The general was determined to defend Crown and Parliament from what he always saw as the unreasonable resistance of colonies that did not seem to accept their own inferior position. Perhaps because he was a bureaucrat who was most happy presiding over clear lines of authority, he was a centralizer. He hoped that the Crown would assume direct control of the four remaining colonies—Pennsylvania, Maryland, Connecticut, and Rhode Island—that were not yet royal provinces. He also wanted to reform all colonial governments, making them more efficient and less recalcitrant. In particular, he hoped to do away with the old requisition system. Before 1763, whenever the king needed support from the colonies he went to each separate assembly to request contributions to his coffers. This system—if one could even call it a system—was slow and cumbersome and always hobbled the military's ability to get money, soldiers, and supplies even during wartime. In time of peace, legislators were still less forthcoming. Although they never directly refused the king's requests, they seldom managed to give the monarch exactly what he asked for. Thus Gage heartily approved of the efforts of Grenville and Townshend to tax the colonies directly, even as he grew increasingly frustrated with a government that seemed incapable of securing obedience to its own laws. Long before Parliament passed the infamous Coercive Acts in 1774, Gage had advised the home government to arrest colonial dissidents and send them to London for trial. He had also advocated the abolition of Boston town meetings and had implied that press censorship would produce salutary results.[37]

Gage had begun to realize just how weak England's position was during the Stamp Act crisis. He had stood by helplessly as demonstrators throughout the colonies took to the streets in opposition to the stamp tax. It was illegal for the army to suppress riots unless civilian leaders asked for help. Unfortunately, colonial governors were reluctant to seek military aid, thus making it impossible to meet "force with force." As early as 1766, Gage was seeing anti-tax protests as "the forerunners of open Rebellion."[38] With the repeal of the Stamp Act, evidence as he saw it of Parliament's remarkable and ill-advised moderation, Gage hoped that imperial disagreements might abate. Instead, the more protracted quarrel over the Townshend Duties meant that he would be even more involved in the political arena.

In 1768, in response to ongoing unrest and threats of violence in Boston, Lord Hillsborough ordered Gage to send troops to the Massachusetts capital. Gage was eager to comply. "It is highly Necessary," he explained, "to retrieve the Dignity of Government which is fallen very low indeed: And the Cause of Britain Should be Supported with Spirit and Vigour."[39] But if the General hoped for spirited and vigorous action, he was destined to be disappointed. The "feeble" attempts to secure the safety of those colonists who ran afoul of the mob made a mockery of British rule. "The Friends of Great Britain, and Government," Gage observed, "are almost afraid to speak, and even the Offices of the Crown grow more timid."[40] In 1770, when Parliament repealed nearly all the Townshend Duties and withdrew troops from Boston as well, Gage was convinced that a chance to defend Parliament's rights had been lost, perhaps for good.

By 1770, Gage and Franklin were on the opposite side of virtually every issue. If Gage thought that His Majesty had every right to send troops any place on the American continent, and only complained when he did not have enough soldiers to get the job done, Franklin was arguing that quartering troops in time of peace was a threat to liberty and should be illegal.[41] While the general thought that the colonies should express their gratitude to Parliament for repealing most of the Townshend Duties, Franklin was urging his compatriots to continue boycotting British goods so long as the tax on tea remained on the books.[42] And at the very time that Thomas Gage was begging the government at home to punish merchants who refused to carry British imports on their ships, Benjamin Franklin was congratulating himself for his part in discouraging Parliament from heeding the general's pleas.[43]

Franklin and Gage were both looking at events from their respective sides of the Atlantic with jaundiced eyes. Each had begun to see corruption and bad faith where they were, even as they tended to view circumstances at home through rose-colored glasses. Thus, although most of his English friends assured Franklin that, after the repeal of the Townshend Acts, Parliament was determined "to be upon good Terms with the Colonies," and that even if the government refused to give up the right to tax it would never actually exercise that right, he was still worried. He believed that most people in England remained friendly to America, but he admitted that there was "a Malice against us in some powerful People, that discovers itself in all their Expressions when they speak of us; And Incidents may yet arise on either Side of the Water that may give them an Advantage."[44] If Franklin saw "Malice" in London, Gage insisted that ever since the "precipitate and Hasty repeal" of the Stamp Act the colonists had become more and more aggressive in their pursuit of a constantly growing list of rights. Especially in Massachusetts, he insisted, the inhabitants had "near annihilated all the Authority of the British Legislature over the Colonies."[45] If this was not independence, it was as close to that undesirable end as Gage ever wanted to get. Thus, Gage was not surprised when the Massachusetts Assembly responded so vituperatively to Governor Hutchinson's valiant attempt to maintain the proper relationship between England and its colonies. The Bay Colony lawmakers had been expanding their own powers for nearly a decade, and no one had done anything serious to rein them in. As Gage saw it, the lower house had "now thrown off all Dependence upon the Supreme Legislature, and done it deliberately, without being prompted to it by any Sudden Heat or Passion."[46]

In the winter of 1773, Gage made plans to leave for England. He looked forward to a long—perhaps a permanent—respite from colonial affairs. Perhaps he would manage, as usual with his brother's help, to obtain a pleasant sinecure, spending the remainder of his life far from the quarrels that had made the last few years so difficult. He surely thought he deserved it.[47] As he watched Wedderburn at the Cockpit, in January 1774, Gage enjoyed a moment of satisfaction. Unlike Lord Hillsborough, he had no personal animus against Franklin, but he knew Thomas Hutchinson and he knew Boston. He was more than pleased to discover that there was someone in London who did not hesitate to defend the king's and Parliament's authority. If that defense had to come at the expense of Benjamin Franklin, so be it.

Of all the observers of Franklin's ordeal at the Cockpit, Edmund Burke was probably the most uncomfortable. He surely winced as Wedderburn "uttered a furious Philippic against poor Dr. Franklin." The solicitor's "invective" was, he thought, "beyond all bounds and measure."[48] Moreover, Burke agreed with Franklin and his lawyer when they argued that there was no good reason for even holding the hearing. "It did not," he insisted, "seem absolutely necessary from the Nature of the Case that there should be any publick Trial whatsoever."[49] The Massachusetts Assembly had asked the king to remove Governor Hutchinson from office. It was the king, not the Privy Council, who should have responded to that request. While it was within the purview of the council to offer its advice to the king, the council had all the information it needed to do its job. Nor was an issue of criminality at stake. Why, he wondered, did either side require a lawyer at all? Obviously, he believed, this meeting was called for political, not legal reasons.[50] And yet, although his description of the "real" reasons for the exhibition at the Cockpit was more-or-less accurate, it is fair to argue that Edmund Burke understood less about the state of imperial affairs, and about Benjamin Franklin's opinions on those affairs, than anyone in the room.

Burke was something of a provincial who, like Franklin, tended to view the English government from the perspective of an outsider. Both men's admiration of all things English knew no bounds. Yet they were skeptical—and perhaps a little envious—of those who took their position in London's inner circles more or less for granted. Burke was a Dubliner. Although his father was a prosperous lawyer and a member of the Church of Ireland, his mother remained a Roman Catholic. To make matters worse, his wife, Jane Mary Nugent, was the daughter of a Catholic physician. Thus the taint of popery, not to mention the whiff of inferiority that came with his Irish background, followed him

Edmund Burke after James Barry, 1774–1775. © National Portrait Gallery, London.

no matter how high he managed to climb. Even some modern histori-ans refer to him disdainfully as an "Irish adventurer" or a "parvenu."[51] Perhaps for that reason, Burke seemed to attract those men who were able to rise on their own merits. His career was surely designed to give someone like Benjamin Franklin a sense that he, too, despite his lowly origins, might be able to attain position and influence in London.[52]

Burke's education was solid if slightly eccentric. He attended Abraham Shackleton's Quaker school as a young boy before entering Trinity College, Dublin. After his graduation in 1748, he briefly stud-ied law at London's Middle Temple before deciding that the legal pro-fession was not to his liking. Instead, he decided to try to earn a living with his pen. He published *A Philosophical Enquiry into the Origin of Our Ideas of the Sublime and Beautiful* in 1757, and the following year he embarked upon an ambitious—and ultimately unfinished—history of England that would begin with Julius Caesar's invasion and end with the reign of Queen Anne.

Perhaps he simply got bogged down in an interminable project, or perhaps he discovered that politics, not writing, was his true vocation. In any event, with the help of his cousin William he became a private secretary for William Gerard Hamilton, Chief Secretary for Ireland, a post he held for three years. In 1765, he assumed the same position for the Marquis of Rockingham, who had just replaced Grenville as the king's chief minister. In December of that year, Burke, himself, became a member of the House of Commons representing the pocket borough of Wendover. He immediately associated himself with the Rockingham Whigs, easily adopting the faction's distrust of the monarchy and never really deviating from that perspective.

As an agent for the colony of New York from 1770 until 1775 Burke, like Franklin, deplored Lord Hillsborough's refusal to accept the credentials of men whose authority came from the assemblies alone. He was aware that the secretary contended that serving at the behest of all three branches of government would "add to the weight and Authority" of colonial agents, but he disagreed. Instead, he insisted that he would only consent to represent the assembly's interests. What, he presciently asked, would an agent do if the lower house asked him to "make complaints" against the governor for "Maladministration of his Office"? How could any assembly trust an agent who owed his position in part to the other two branches of government? If New Yorkers disapproved of his stance, he said, he would gladly resign his position. But of course that never happened.[53]

Burke was nothing if not charming. Moreover, he was an accomplished orator at a time when rhetorical skill truly mattered. Still, his enemies were many, and they were merciless in their attacks on his character. They found it difficult to see a thread of consistency in his speeches, contending that as a perennial member of the opposition, he exploited whatever issue that arose, adroitly twisting it to suit his own ends.[54] Thomas Hutchinson, for one, did not trust him at all, insisting that Burke's "flowered" oratory and his "great verbosity" led his handful of admirers to forget that he was a man of no substance. Burke, claimed Hutchinson, was good at criticizing others, but had no constructive ideas of his own. No matter what he said to the contrary, he did not even sympathize with American ideals. He was simply using the differences dividing the Empire to bring down whatever administration happened to be in power at the moment.[55]

It was easy for many to dismiss Burke as a mere troublemaker. Because he eschewed theoretical analyses of rights in favor of practical solutions, he may have looked like a man who had no real principles. In fact, however, his perspective on the Empire was remarkably consistent—more consistent, in fact, than Benjamin Franklin's. As was the case for so many people on both sides of the Atlantic, Burke's introduction to imperial affairs came as Parliament struggled over the repeal of the Stamp Act. At first the new ministry hoped to avoid discussion of the Stamp Act altogether. When it finally became convinced that it was impossible to force the colonies to obey the act, Rockingham's supporters began searching for a face-saving way to get rid of the problematic legislation once and for all. They did their best to avoid constitutional issues and to make their case solely on pragmatic economic grounds. Thus, even before news of a colonial boycott of British goods reached London, Rockingham urged the English merchants to begin a campaign to repeal the Stamp Act. Still, the administration always believed that the government did need to save face. Consequently, it devised the Declaratory Act, which proclaimed that Parliament had the unquestioned right to legislate for the colonies "in all cases whatsoever." To Burke—indeed to most Englishmen—this was simply stating the obvious. English history proved that, ever since the revolutionary settlement of 1689, Parliament was sovereign. Its legislative (which would include taxation) powers were unlimited. Although he thought it would be unwise to tax the colonies in the future, Burke never argued that Parliament did not have the right to do just that. That this position was virtually identical with the views of Thomas Hutchinson never seemed to cross his mind.

When Benjamin Franklin appeared before Parliament to testify against the Stamp Act in 1766, he did not directly take issue with Burke's perspective. True enough, he pointed out that virtually no one in America believed that Parliament had the right to tax the colonies. Nevertheless, he thought that most people would be willing to ignore the Declaratory Act once the Stamp Act was gone. Like Burke, he was willing to concentrate not on Parliament's theoretical claims to power but on what the English government actually planned to do. Nearly a decade later, as he stood silently at the Cockpit, Franklin thought that he had been wrong to be so optimistic.

In 1774 Burke still stood solidly behind the principles animating the Declaratory Act, even as he argued vigorously that Parliament should not exercise the very right to tax that it clearly had. He had opposed the Townshend Duties, seeing them as—if anything— counterproductive. They did not promise much in the way of badly needed revenue. Worse, they had forced the colonists into an increasingly belligerent stance, endangering an Empire that as early as 1770 Burke described as "crumbling" and "tottering."[56] When Parliament repealed most of Townshend's legislation, Burke had been pleased, but he failed to understand why Lord North insisted on retaining what Burke saw as an economically useless but politically explosive tax on tea. He did not arrive at this position on principle; rather he thought it was simply a foolish gesture that would cause nothing but trouble. He knew that whenever Parliament emphasized its right to tax, the colonists became ever more suspicious and ever more determined to defend their "rights" and to question imperial authority.

Nor was Burke impressed with arguments from growing numbers of Members of Parliament that Parliament was digging its own grave whenever it backed down in the face of colonial complaints. He did not agree with Thomas Gage that the government was encouraging disobedience and even independence by attempting to mollify people who would never be satisfied. The repeal of the Stamp Act, Gage said, had led Americans to believe that all they had to do was protest, and they would have their way. Like spoiled children, they stamped their feet and refused to obey the most reasonable laws or to pay the least onerous of taxes. Never grateful for Parliament's mercy, they always wanted more. Burke contended that just the opposite was true. The more we "refuse to gratify" the colonists, he declared, the more radical they become.[57] If we quit trying to tax them, they would have nothing more to protest. And thus the Empire would be saved.

Burke invariably tried to avoid "metaphysical" discussions of abstract rights. Words such as "prudence" and "expedience" dotted his prose, as he begged his colleagues to abandon a path that he was convinced would lead to the destruction of the Empire. "Profitable experience," not "mischievous theory," should be the guiding light.[58] Talk of rights, he insisted, merely inflamed minds. It did not solve problems.

Instead, he urged England to return to the policies it had followed without serious difficulty before 1763. Parliament should abandon the "ground of difference," be content with regulating trade for the good of the Empire as a whole, and let each colonial government tax itself, voluntarily complying with the king's requests. If Parliament truly wanted the colonies to be useful to England, then it was "a little preposterous to make them unserviceable in order to keep them obedient."[59] No matter what its intentions, he thought, the government was in danger of losing both its own rights and its control of the colonies.

Burke seemed not to recognize that by 1774 almost no one, on either side of the Atlantic, accepted his understanding of imperial issues. Parliament was determined to assert its right to tax the colonies, and it would listen to no one who argued that there were times when lawmakers were wise to avoid doing something, even if they had the right to do it. Americans were equally intent upon claiming their right to legislate for and to tax themselves, and they no longer trusted the assurances of their dwindling number of English friends who insisted that Parliament had no desire to destroy colonial liberties. To the contrary, the colonists' understanding of their rights was moving in a direction that Burke would never countenance. They were no longer demanding the "rights of Englishmen" but were talking instead of universal "natural rights." Burke, however, did not seem to realize that his defense of the colonies was no longer adequate to the occasion.[60]

In 1766 Benjamin Franklin had been willing to overlook Parliament's claims to sovereignty as he sought a practical resolution to the quarrels that threatened to divide the Empire. But in 1774 he insisted upon England's complete recognition of colonial rights. When Burke claimed that Parliament had the right to tax the colonies, but that it should simply desist from doing so, Franklin staunchly disagreed. At one time, he—like the vast majority of colonial Americans—would have been happy enough to have returned to English practice as it had existed before 1763. Now, however, independence seemed to be the only viable option.

Thomas Hutchinson, of course, was not present at the Cockpit. He was still in Massachusetts, winding up his personal affairs, preparing to travel to London for what he hoped would be a brief sojourn.

Nevertheless, his spirit hovered over the proceedings. No one forgot for a moment that it was Hutchinson's struggles as governor of the Bay Colony that were in large part responsible for Franklin's Cockpit ordeal.

In so many ways, Thomas Hutchinson and Benjamin Franklin were very much alike. Both were native Bostonians, of course. In fact Hutchinson, whose ancestors had been members of the Bay Colony's founding generation, had much longer and deeper ties to Massachusetts than Franklin did. And they were roughly contemporaries— Franklin was only five years older than the governor. Both were solid defenders of colonial rights, even as they were staunch Empire men. Hutchinson never abandoned his assumption that America's fortunes depended upon a strong connection to England. But until very late in the game, Franklin thought much the same thing, although he envisioned a more equal partnership between England and its colonies than the governor did.

In temperament, too, the two men were surprisingly similar. They were prudent and cautious rather than rash and ideological. While Hutchinson never abandoned the congregational church into which he was born, he—like Franklin—was a religious moderate who disliked disputes over theological niceties and thought all religions should be judged by their practical effects. Both men were invariably uncomfortable with extremes. They were, for instance, almost equally dismayed by colonial violence during the Stamp Act crisis. And although they enjoyed considerable material success, and could easily afford the finest accouterments, they tended toward genteel modesty. When Hutchinson bowed to the importunities of his friends and bought a coach, he purchased a second-hand vehicle, and he did even that with great reluctance.[61] Similarly, Franklin bragged that long after he could afford to do otherwise, he and Deborah "kept no idle Servants, our Table was plain & simple, our Furniture of the cheapest."[62]

Franklin and Hutchinson were not simply temperamentally compatible. In less rancorous times they had actually worked with one another and supported one another. Both men could point with pride to the efforts they had made to strengthen the Empire. Hutchinson had labored almost as hard in Massachusetts as Franklin had done in Pennsylvania to secure financing for the French and Indian War. In 1754, as the colonies faced the very real prospect of hostilities with their French neighbors, the two met in Albany, New York, where they combined their talents to devise the ill-fated Albany Plan of Union. The plan called for the creation of a government composed of representatives from every province that would be in charge of defending the colonies from the incursions of the French and their Indian allies. Unfortunately, almost no one, not king, not Parliament, not the colonial legislatures, was interested in a plan that would, however lightly, impinge upon their own prerogatives. Both men had been disappointed at the reception their proposal garnered, and both had chafed at the colonial provincialism that rendered it impossible for any colony to support the flimsiest continental government.

Significantly, it was to Franklin that Hutchinson turned when he endured one of the most painful experiences of his public life. Thomas Hutchinson had not been a proponent of the Stamp Act. To the contrary, he had lobbied diligently for the act's repeal. But he could not countenance outright disobedience to the legislation so long as it was in effect. His enemies—and he had many—found such fine distinctions unacceptable. They already distrusted him, due to his uncanny, some said suspicious, ability to garner political plums for himself and his family at a time when government patronage was difficult to secure. Thus they were convinced that he was using his nuanced position to curry favor with English officialdom so that he could garner even more royal favors in the years to come. Even so, most Bostonians were stunned by the fate that befell him on the night of August 26, 1765. He and his family had just sat down to dinner when an axe-wielding mob stormed the house, tearing down curtains and pictures, shattering china, and cleaving furniture into bits. His books, papers, and clothes were either destroyed on the spot or carried outside where they were trampled in the mud or left to drift aimlessly in the wind. In all, Hutchinson lost goods worth 2,500 pounds sterling that night. He and his children managed—just barely—to escape before the rioters could do them any physical harm. But the emotional scars of the experience never healed. Hutchinson sought compensation for his losses. He wrote to his old friend, Benjamin Franklin, for help in seeing that his pleas navigated London's cumbersome governmental bureaucracy. Just as Franklin had sympathized with Lord North when he was the victim of John Wilkes's mobs, he was appalled by Hutchinson's treatment in Boston.

Still, despite their similarities, Benjamin Franklin and Thomas Hutchinson were profoundly different. Ironically, Hutchinson was more of an American than his cosmopolitan counterpart. While Franklin's father was an immigrant, Hutchinson's ancestors had helped settle Massachusetts, and the governor was always proud of his deep and abiding familial connections to the Bay Colony's history. When he was forced into exile in 1774, he was disconsolate. Franklin had thrived in England's capital, enjoying a rich and satisfying social life there, but Hutchinson never quite felt at home in this alien land, and he always looked forward to returning to the place of his birth. "I am an American," he told a friend. Although everyone urged him to settle permanently in England, he admitted that he could not "give up the hopes of laying my bones in New England; and hitherto I consider myself as only upon an excursion from home." Despite the fact that so many in England embraced him when he arrived in the nation's capital, he told his daughter that "I had rather live at Milton than Kew."[63]

If Hutchinson pined for America, he longed even more to be close to all the members of his extended family. Franklin was not much of a family man. He was fond of Deborah and remained a dutiful, if distant, father to his daughter, Sally. Until the mid-seventies he was especially close to his son William. Still, he was perfectly content to stay away from home for years on end, kindly but firmly rejecting Deborah's increasingly desperate pleas for his return to Philadelphia. Hutchinson, on the other hand, lived for his family. It was the very center of his life. So long as he was surrounded by his children and their spouses, he was happy. Indeed, he preferred an insular life, shutting out strangers and acquaintances, and listening only to those who probably agreed with him already.[64]

Perhaps because he conferred so often with his own kind, Hutchinson tended to be more inflexible than Franklin. Franklin at least considered all viewpoints, and he was even known to change his mind when presented with persuasive evidence. He knew where the political winds blew, and he was willing to move in the right direction. Hutchinson, however, for all his moderation, was more principled, more rigid, more determined to defend his perspective no matter what the consequences to himself or his cause might be. Unfortunately for him, for Franklin, and for the Empire he cherished, it was his adherence to his principles that ultimately led to the showdown at the Cockpit.

CHAPTER 3

·····················

Errata

W hy, his friends wondered at the time, and historians have wondered ever since, had the politically savvy Benjamin Franklin made so colossal a blunder? How could he possibly have believed that throwing the red meat contained in the Hutchinson/Oliver letters to an already hostile Massachusetts Assembly would ease tensions between England and America? The idea seems so preposterous on the face of it, that many observers—then and now—take it for granted that Wedderburn was right when he accused Franklin of knowing full well what the results of his grand gesture would be. Others, just as nonplussed, take him at his word. They simply shrug their shoulders and confess that in this case, the usually astute Franklin had miscalculated—that he had made a huge, uncharacteristic, and extremely costly mistake.

We will probably never know whether or not Franklin actually understood the implications of what he was doing when he forwarded those letters to Thomas Cushing, although it is worth noting that he never deviated from his explanation of his motives. One thing, however, is clear. If Franklin did, however wrongly, believe that his actions would bring peace to the Empire it was by no means the first time that he had been the victim of his own lack of judgment. Indeed, his *Autobiography* is riddled with accounts of the various "errata" that dotted his personal life throughout his formative years. That same *Autobiography*, however, invariably made light of Franklin's mistakes. Every printer knew, of course, that errors were common, virtually unavoidable, and that an "errata page" at the end of a book or magazine would make everything right. And in his own life, Franklin very carefully noted not only the mistakes he made but also the ways he managed to correct them. Some of his missteps were personal and private, affecting only him and the men and women closest to him. Others, especially in the 1760s and 1770s, were public, political, and very costly. Clearly, Franklin was not always the shrewd political operator or the excellent judge of character of popular myth. In this sense, his failure to appreciate the ramifications of his decision to send the Hutchinson/Oliver letters to Massachusetts was no anomaly. It was par for the course.

We tend to see Franklin as the quintessential example of the American success story, in large part because his *Autobiography* very deliberately leads us to do so. Looked at one way, his life was the stuff of which the Horatio Alger myth is made. Franklin was the poor boy made good. He was the son of Josiah Franklin, Boston candle-maker, and Abiah Folger, former indentured servant. Reared in "poverty and obscurity," he eventually rose, through hard work, determination, and native intelligence, to "a State of Affluence and some Degree of Reputation in the World."[1] While the *Autobiography* admits to an occasional mistake in its author's rise to the top, it depicts none of Franklin's errata as venal or even particularly unintelligent. As Franklin tells it, most of his errors in judgment were minor, generally the result of pardonable naiveté. Moreover, they usually led to something good in the end. If, however, readers take a step back and look at Franklin's life from a less credulous perspective, they might be surprised to see just how wrong Franklin often was, how many failures and near calamities he brought upon himself, and how close he came to destroying his own political career before he managed to regain his footing and start—or restart—his climb to the top. It can easily be argued that, first in his personal life, then as a political animal, Franklin made more than his fair share of costly errors.

Franklin was not completely exaggerating when he said that his beginnings were inauspicious. True enough, he was born a respectable member of Boston's artisan community. And while he received only two years of formal schooling before entering the working world at the age of ten, his parents were literate, his father owned his own business, and he had no real fear that he would ever sink to the level of the "poorer sort," the day laborers, servants, and beggars who were becoming ever more visible throughout urban America by the middle of the eighteenth century. When he was twelve, Franklin signed on to work as an apprentice in his brother James's printing shop. He would later complain about the "harsh and tyrannical Treatment" he endured there, even as—predictably—he claimed that his sufferings were a blessing in disguise. They gave him, he later said, "the Aversion to arbitrary Power" that would inform his perspective on the world for the rest of his life.[2] Although he seemed loath to admit it, Franklin gained much more from his brother than the tendency to hate capricious authority. He learned the printer's trade. He honed his skills as a reader and a writer, slipping some of his own witty pieces into James's newspaper, the *New England Courant*, under a pseudonym. He also met and rubbed shoulders with some of the most outspoken critics of Boston's hidebound ways. When the "tyrannical" James ran afoul of the town's authorities and was consequently forbidden from publishing his paper, Benjamin was presented with the opportunity to flee both Boston and his brother. To keep the *Courant* in business, James hit upon what looked like a brilliant subterfuge. He put his paper in Benjamin's name, publicly tearing up his brother's apprenticeship, even as he secretly drew up a second indenture that replicated the provisions of the first. Benjamin shrewdly took advantage of James's awkward position, knowing that his brother could not possibly let his own illicit maneuverings see the light of day. And thus he ran away, eventually landing in Philadelphia, leaving James and the *Courant* in the lurch.

As Franklin later told the story, his rise to the top commenced almost as soon as he entered Pennsylvania's capital city. Exaggerating his poverty in those early days, and carefully downplaying the advantages he had—the ability to read and write, a marketable skill, good references, friends and family back home to whom he could turn if he failed—he implied that he succeeded on his own, that he was, indeed, a self-made man. He also depicted his acquisition of fame and fortune as virtually inevitable. The reality was quite different. Franklin floundered for years. He may have been ambitious, but he was driven by no particular goal. Worse, what appeared to him to be excellent opportunities for advancement often turned into unmitigated disasters, in many cases due to his own incredibly poor judgment. Indeed, Franklin's early failures foreshadow the stops and starts that characterized his personal and public life at least until 1774. Ironically, his superior intellect was at least partly responsible for many of his missteps. Able to do almost everything he tried, supremely self-confident, overly optimistic, he simply could not imagine that he could fail.

When he arrived in Philadelphia, Franklin accepted a job with printer Samuel Keimer. Almost immediately, he began criticizing his new boss, chafing at Keimer's eccentric habits, convinced—at the ripe old age of eighteen—that he could do better. Consequently, when Pennsylvania governor William Keith praised him as "a young Man of Promising Parts" and offered to set him up in business, Franklin was delighted.[3] His father wisely urged him to think again, observing that his son was much "too young to be trusted with the Management of a Business so important."[4] Undaunted and clearly basking in the governor's fulsome praise, young Franklin forged ahead. He was thrilled when Keith suggested that he should sail to England with the governor's letters of credit, valuable papers that would enable him to purchase all the supplies he needed to open his own shop. Despite the fact that Keith never seemed to find the time to give him the papers he had promised, Franklin embarked for London in 1724. It never occurred to him that his benefactor would fail him. Indeed, he was convinced that a packet he saw in the possession of the ship's captain contained the precious documents he needed. Only when he arrived at his destination did he realize that he had been duped. Everyone but Franklin it turned out knew that Keith could not be trusted, that he was "liberal of Promises which he never meant to keep." A typical politician, he "wish'd to please every body; and having little to give, he gave Expectations." Franklin was angry at a man who would play "such pitiful Tricks" on a "poor ignorant Boy."[5] But his father had warned him that this might happen, and anyone in Philadelphia could have told him the same thing had he been willing to listen. Franklin's first effort to set himself up as an independent businessman ended in failure, the result of his own credulity and his inflated sense of his own self-worth.

Thus he found himself in a city whose size made Philadelphia look like a mere village. He had no connections, no job, no money. He managed to gain employment at a printer's shop, but he was clearly not committed to the only career for which his skills and experience had prepared him. All of London lay before him. "Plays and other Places of Amusement" occupied his spare time and ate up his paltry earnings, and he lived from "hand to mouth" so long as he remained in England.[6] If an older and wiser Franklin would advise his readers that a penny saved was a penny earned, young Benjamin readily succumbed to the temptations of England's metropolis. Nor did he have any idea what he wanted to do with the rest of his life. He thought seriously about staying in England and becoming a swimming teacher. But ultimately he returned to Philadelphia, not as a printer, but as a clerk in a friend's store. When his new boss died, however, he was jobless yet again. Hat in hand, he asked Keimer to take him on once more, and despite the shabby treatment he had received from his former employee, Keimer consented. Franklin was right back where he had been when he first arrived in Pennsylvania. He had nothing to show for his efforts but a bruised ego and some exciting adventures he could embellish with fondness in his old age.

Finally Franklin began to turn his life around, although his success was at least partly the result of luck rather than pluck. His relations with Keimer were, if anything, worse than they had been before he left for England. Things got so bad, that he considered giving up completely, returning to Boston and admitting defeat. Instead, Hugh Meredith, a fellow apprentice, persuaded him to remain in Philadelphia. Once Hugh had completed his terms of apprenticeship, his father set the two young men up in their own print shop. Two years later, when it became obvious that Meredith was a mediocre printer and a hopeless drunk to boot, Franklin—with the help of friends who loaned him the money—bought the shop from Hugh's father and abandoned his former partner. In 1730, seven years after he had first set foot in his new home, he was at last on his way to becoming his own master.

Franklin's prospects also benefited from an advantageous marriage. When he first arrived in Philadelphia, he boarded with artisan John Read. It was not long before Franklin and Read's daughter, Deborah, formed an attachment. Fate and the fickleness of youth intervened. Before Benjamin left for London on his fool's errand, he and Deborah "interchang'd some promises" but did not marry.[7] Once in England, Franklin seemed to have forgotten all about his fiancée. Feeling abandoned, Deborah married John Rogers, an abusive husband who eventually deserted her. By the time Franklin returned to Philadelphia, Deborah was "dejected, and seldom cheerful, and avoided Company."[8]

Although he knew that he was largely responsible for Deborah's misfortunes, Franklin nevertheless sought a lucrative union elsewhere. To put the matter bluntly, he hoped to marry someone whose family could provide him with a dowry of at least 100 pounds, the sum he needed to pay his outstanding debts. Unfortunately for him, however, no matter how confident he was of his own worth, most people did not think highly of his material prospects. He was forced to admit, after a couple of failed attempts, that he "was not to expect Money with a Wife."[9] By this time, he was desperate. Having "frequently" indulged in "Intrigues with low Women" upon his return to Philadelphia, he was about to become a father.[10] Deborah was in no position to drive a hard bargain. She was a good woman, a hard worker, and she agreed to raise William, who was born in 1731, as her own son. Franklin could not help but congratulate himself on a good outcome for what had been an extremely messy process, noting that, however belatedly, he had corrected another erratum.[11]

In fact, his marriage turned out to be extremely advantageous to Benjamin Franklin. He made good use of the half lot on Market Street that Deborah inherited from her father. More importantly, his wife was a native Philadelphian with excellent connections to many important families in town. Her best friend, for instance, was the sister of Isaac Norris, Speaker of the Pennsylvania Assembly. As her husband's reputation grew and he found himself on the road more and more often, it was Deborah who kept the family business afloat. After 1757, when Franklin crossed the Atlantic for a second time, returning home only briefly before leaving for London yet again, Deborah's services were essential. She took care of Benjamin's correspondence, managed his accounts, supervised the construction of their new house, and secured tenants for the family's rental property. She was one of her husband's best sources for news from home, even as she kept Franklin's Philadelphia friends apprised of his comings and goings. Franklin may have backed into his marriage, having taken more detours along the way than most men did, but he could not—or should not—have denied that Deborah was essential to his success both at home and abroad.

Unknown Artist, *Deborah Franklin*, 1759. American Philosophical Society.

Indeed, the printing establishment on Market Street, once it got off the ground, was a resounding success, as was its owner. Franklin quickly made up for lost time. He was the instigator of a series of projects designed to improve his adopted home. The lending library, fire company, city hospital, College of Philadelphia, and American Philosophical Society all owed their existence to the unflagging public spirit of Benjamin Franklin. He was a scientist as well as a reformer. While he was fascinated by problems that were of no immediate practical value, he was especially pleased when his experiments resulted in something useful. He counted among his proudest achievements the invention of bifocals, the glass armonica, and the Franklin stove. And of course he garnered international fame for his lightning rod, a device that tamed the lightning, dramatically cutting down the number of fires that were the scourge of city dwellers everywhere. Franklin did much more than his share to make the world in which he lived a better place. He also improved his own prospects. His *Pennsylvania Gazette* and, even more, his *Poor Richard's Almanac* were wildly popular, giving him a reputation for wit and intelligence as well as good business sense. He bought and sold property and, with the help of his wife and mother-in-law, earned a tidy sum from the little shop located next to his home. He sponsored printing establishments in other colonies, generally taking one-third of the profits in exchange for providing printers the equipment they needed to get started. He owned rental property, dabbled in real estate and land speculation, and owned a number of paper mills.[12] Once he got started, he took advantage of every opportunity. He used his appointment as clerk of the Pennsylvania Assembly, for instance, to secure the job as official printer for the colony's lawmakers. And almost before he knew it, he was the printer for Delaware, New Jersey, and Maryland. By the time he retired at the age of forty-two, he was a wealthy man.

But wealth in colonial America did not always bring status. There were some things even Benjamin Franklin could not do and some places he could not go. When, as he ruefully put it, he "try'd a little" to fill the office of justice of the peace, he had to concede that he did not have the legal knowledge to do the job properly.[13] And while the members of the respectable middle class were proud to count him as one of their own, Philadelphia's true elite saw him as nothing more than the upstart printer that he was. Self-made men may have become admirable in America by the nineteenth century. In Franklin's day, a man with low beginnings who worked with his hands was not to be trusted. It was only in 1748, when he sold his print shop and declared his independence from the day-to-day grind, that some people in Philadelphia began to see him as a potential leader.

Franklin's early errors in judgment were both forgivable and understandable. His mistakes were private; they only affected him or those like James and Deborah who were closest to him. He may have vacillated a bit more than most men. But perhaps that was because he was so talented and seemed to have so many options. Beginning in the late

1750s, Franklin's occasional tendency to overestimate his own abilities and, even worse, to misunderstand the political realities he faced had significant consequences for him, for Pennsylvania, and even for the colonies as a whole. His misguided campaign to make Pennsylvania a royal colony is a case in point.

In 1757 Benjamin Franklin was fifty-one years old. He was respected in Philadelphia and had even made something of a name for himself at the continental level. The Crown had appointed him, along with William Hunter of Virginia, deputy postmasters general for the colonies in 1753, thus making him the proud holder of a lucrative royal sinecure. His position gave him an excuse to travel throughout America, meeting the movers and shakers of the provincial world. In the process, he gained a reputation as a hard worker, a shrewd organizer, and a convivial companion. A year later, he was Pennsylvania's delegate to the Albany Conference. That both England and the colonies ignored his Albany Plan of Union was almost beside the point. Its very existence signaled to those who were paying attention that Benjamin Franklin's interests were not confined to Pennsylvania affairs.

Still, it was in Pennsylvania that Franklin truly shined. By 1757 he had every right to think that he had played his cards wisely. Six years earlier he had been elected for the first time to the colony's assembly, a position he held for the next decade. He quickly allied himself with, and indeed became the moving force behind, what contemporaries called the "Quaker Party," although, in part due to Franklin's nudging, the faction became increasingly secular. Its unifying principle centered on its members' opposition to the rule of Pennsylvania Proprietors Thomas and Richard Penn, the Anglican sons of the colony's revered founder, Quaker William Penn. The Penns took their responsibilities—and even more their rights—seriously. They were the Crown-appointed owners of one of the most prosperous of England's mainland colonies, and they thought it only just that they should reap significant financial rewards from Pennsylvania. Thus, even in a time of war when the cost of defending the colony dramatically increased, they refused to allow the assembly to tax their own vast estates. They were not represented in the lower house, they always pointed out, and hence they could not be taxed.

The Penns, especially Thomas, had what many in the colony considered inflated notions of their own power. They repeatedly bound the governors they appointed with rigid—and secret—instructions, giving them no flexibility and little room to compromise. Because governors who deviated from the Penns' instructions faced dismissal, they all vetoed assembly legislation—especially when it included efforts to tax the Proprietors' land—with increasing regularity. That the Penns had every right to issue their instructions, and that the king himself was doing the same thing in the far more numerous royal colonies, was, as members of the Pennsylvania Assembly saw it, irrelevant. They believed that they were the victims of rapacious and dictatorial rulers who cared little for the welfare of the inhabitants over whom they ruled with a heavy hand.

The root cause of all the differences dividing the Proprietors from the Quaker Party was their diametrically opposed understandings of the rights and powers of the assembly. Almost as soon as Pennsylvania had been founded, the lower house began to demand what it believed were its rights. Members wanted the power to initiate legislation, to appoint judges in good behavior, and to be called into session at regular intervals. Above all, they demanded the right to tax and to decide how the revenue they raised would be spent. They conceived of themselves, in other words, as a miniature parliament. The Penns, on the other hand, were convinced that the assembly was trying to destroy their own legitimate exercise of power altogether, thus turning Pennsylvania into a headless republic. Neither side was really interested in compromise, and thus the quarrels between the assembly and the Proprietors escalated.

In the beginning, Franklin had been a conciliator. He did not like the Penns, but neither was he always happy with the Quaker Party. The Quakers refused to spend any money on what they defined as "offensive war." They were almost as reluctant to do much to defend the colony from attack. Certainly no pacifist, Franklin understood the anger and fear of Pennsylvania's western settlers who felt threatened by hostile Indians. He was also a stalwart supporter of England's almost continuous wars against France. And he was amazingly adept at devising ways to get around the assembly's refusal to allocate funds for King George's War (1744–1748) and the French and Indian War (1754–1763), helping to create voluntary militias that would take the place of more regular, tax supported forces.

By 1757, however, Franklin had had enough. He had received little praise for his contributions to the defense of Pennsylvania from

French and Indian attack. He had come to believe that the Penns were acting from "petty private Considerations" and that the governors they appointed were a "Disgrace" who deserved the "Curses of all the Continent."[14] While he disapproved of Quaker pacifism, he was even more frustrated by Proprietary parsimony. Granted, the Penns occasionally contributed a bit from their own coffers to the colony's defense. But, standing on what they saw as their rights, they always insisted upon doing so voluntarily. Thus when Pennsylvania lawmakers asked Franklin to sail for London to persuade the Penns to alter their resistance to the assembly's efforts to tax their land, he eagerly accepted. He and his son set sail in June. William would study law at London's Middle Temple, attaining the legal expertise that his father had never enjoyed. Benjamin would take care of the colony's business in short order.

When Franklin set foot on England's shores, he could not help but contrast his reception with the one he had encountered on his first trip to London. Then he had been a nobody, a penniless and bewildered boy who had struggled to make his way in a harsh and unforgiving world. Now he was a world-renowned scientist with impeccable political credentials and plenty of money in his pockets. Scientists and printers who had once known him only by reputation or through their correspondence now rushed to see him in the flesh. They were immediately taken with a man whose wit and sophistication made him the most excellent of companions. Printer William Strahan echoed the sentiments of many of Franklin's newfound friends when he wrote to Deborah, "I never saw a man who was in every respect, so perfectly agreeable to me. Some are amiable in one view, some in another, he in all."[15]

Relishing such praise, Franklin may have overestimated his own ability to achieve his ends. He was, after all, the man who admitted in his *Autobiography* that he was never able to acquire the virtue of humility, having to content himself with exhibiting the "Appearance" of a trait that he truly admired.[16] He had already come so far. He had employed his intelligence and charm to such good effect in Philadelphia on so many occasions, using the power of reason to overcome the doubts of all but his most obdurate opponents. He may not have been a gifted speaker, but he could craft a written argument as well as anyone and better than most. Moreover, he was convinced that he had justice on his side. Once he explained his position to London's powers-that-be, surely they would see things his way.

Franklin was unprepared for the realities he faced in England's capital. The government bureaucracy there was complicated and unwieldy, difficult for even the most seasoned veterans to navigate. Then, too, if the Philadelphia elite looked upon him with a certain disdain, true aristocrats were even more apt to dismiss him as a colonial upstart. Perhaps most unsettling—although he refused to admit it for over a decade—was the reality that most of England's political leaders shared the perspective of the Penns, not of Benjamin Franklin. They were as troubled as the Proprietors by what they saw as the inflated claims of colonial assemblies. They agreed that Americans needed to be put in their place and to accept their subordinate position in the Empire. Franklin came face-to-face with this view almost as soon as he arrived in London, when he met briefly with Lord Granville, president of the Privy Council. He had been complaining about the Proprietors' instructions to their governors when Granville suddenly interrupted him. The Penns, he lectured, were totally within their rights; indeed the king himself issued instructions to royal governors that had the full force of law and could not be altered by anyone, especially, he implied, a mere colonial assembly. "THE KING," Granville proclaimed, "IS THE LEGISLATOR OF THE COLONIES." Franklin admitted to being more than "a little alarm'd" by his encounter, but he refused to be discouraged or to admit that Granville's view was shared by many.[17]

Undaunted, Franklin went to work. Disregarding the advice of Englishmen who knew how to get things done, he tried to press his case to well-placed members of the ministry, none of whom seemed impressed by his credentials. Most would not even deign to see him. Those who did gave him little hope that his mission would succeed. Thus, in August, he arranged a meeting with Thomas and Richard Penn. Franklin poured on the charm, assuring the Proprietors that no one in Pennsylvania wanted to destroy their power or reduce their profits. The Penns listened attentively and pretended to be willing to consider the assembly's concerns, asking only that Franklin put his requests in writing. Franklin agreed, drawing up something that he called the "Heads of Complaint."

The August meeting was the last reasonably cordial encounter the three men had. Franklin received no official response to his "Heads" for over a year, although he continued to meet privately from time to time with Thomas Penn. Each time the atmosphere grew tenser. In

Unknown Artist, *Thomas Penn Esq.*, n.d. Yale University Art Gallery, Mabel Brady Garvan Collection.

January 1758, the two men almost came to blows. Penn belittled the assembly's claims to legislative authority and, when Franklin pointed out that Penn's own father had recognized those claims, the Proprietor simply sneered. No one, he insisted, not even William Penn, could give colonial assemblies powers to which they had no right. Franklin walked away from the confrontation declaring that he "conceived that Moment a more cordial and thorough Contempt for [Thomas Penn] than I ever before felt for any Man living."[18] If Franklin had harbored any hopes for a friendly relationship with the Proprietors before 1758, he never again believed that the Penns were interested in accommodation. To the contrary, he hoped that the Proprietors would be "gibbeted up as they deserve, to rot and stink in the Nostrils of Posterity."[19]

Refusing to concede defeat, Franklin employed his highly honed literary skills to defend Pennsylvania from newspaper attacks that he was convinced were inspired by the Penns. Writing for the *London Chronicle* and the *Gentleman's Magazine*, he tried to convince readers that the malicious criticisms of his colony were totally without merit. His ambitious *An Historical Review of the Constitution and Government of Pennsylvania* aimed at the same end. But what worked in Pennsylvania, where everyone knew him, and where his intended audience shared his general perspective and was at least willing to consider his arguments, had little impact in London. He may have been talented, but his abilities did not reap the results in England that they had at home. The Proprietors' understanding of their powers was, it turned out, conventional wisdom in London.

In the end, Franklin appealed first to the Board of Trade and then to the Privy Council, hoping to force the Penns to do what they would not voluntarily agree to on their own. The Penns' influence, as well as the pervasive hostility to the pretensions of colonial assemblies, led the Board to reject Franklin's requests outright. Pennsylvania, it said, could not tax the Proprietors' property. Although everyone told him that an appeal to the Privy Council would be useless, Franklin doggedly forged ahead. In the end, he obtained what one historian has aptly labeled a "shallow victory."[20] The council agreed that the assembly could, indeed, tax the Proprietors' unimproved lands, but it could do so only if it assessed those lands at the lowest rates in Pennsylvania. Moreover, the Penns could appeal any assessment they saw as unfair, and they would have a say in the way that their taxes would be spent.

His treatment at the hands of London officialdom should have served as a cautionary tale. That Franklin had managed to get even a tiny portion of what he wanted was nothing short of miraculous. He should have realized that if scientists and printers admired him, government officials were less impressed. Nevertheless, Franklin left for home two years after his appearance before the Privy Council as a man on a mission. He was determined to sever the colony's ties with the Proprietors once and for all. His goal was to turn Pennsylvania into a royal colony.

When Franklin returned to Philadelphia in 1762 he was greeted enthusiastically by his supporters in the Quaker Party. At first, he seemed happy to be home, as he immersed himself once more in the tricky ins and outs of Pennsylvania politics, a task made more difficult than ever by the challenges the Empire faced in a postwar world. If England had emerged victorious from its long and very costly war with France in 1763, it did not take long for some to wonder if success had come at too high a price. The provisions of the Peace of Paris had allowed England to extend its rule over all of the French possessions in Canada. Overnight it assumed the administrative costs of governing a huge new territory inhabited to a large extent by Catholic Frenchmen who had no love for a country with which they had been at war for decades. Moreover, General Jeffrey Amherst, commander of His Majesty's forces in America, was not the only one to warn that the natives in the areas formerly controlled by the French were uneasy and that they would more than likely resist any encroachments on their lands.

Amherst's dire prediction was borne out almost immediately when hostilities broke out between Indians and settlers on Pennsylvania's frontier. The Quaker-dominated assembly grudgingly allocated a modest sum to defend the colony's western inhabitants, but as the frustrated and frightened frontiersmen saw it, the Quakers were more interested in protecting "friendly" Indians than they were in defending white settlers. Nor were settlers in any mood to discriminate between friendly and enemy natives. In December 1763, the "Paxton Boys," as they became known, went on a rampage, massacring twenty innocent natives in Lancaster. Still angry in February, they rode to Philadelphia, threatening to destroy the city if the government refused to hand over some Indian refugees who had fled there for protection. Franklin leapt to the defense of the city, putting aside his hostility to the Penns, perhaps hoping that he would be recognized—even rewarded—for his efforts. He quickly dashed off a pamphlet, *A Narrative of the Late Massacres*, deploring the "brutal undistinguishing Resentment against all Indians, Friends as well as Foes."[21] He also helped raise a large number of volunteers to defend Philadelphia from possible attack.

John Penn, the Proprietors' nephew, was the unfortunate governor at the time. Although Franklin described him as confused, even panicked by the threat posed by the Paxton Boys, Penn actually rose to the occasion. He consulted with governors in the neighboring colonies, requesting a safe haven for Philadelphia's Indian refugees. When the governors refused, he persuaded General Gage to send three battalions

Henry Dawkins, *Paxton Expedition*, Inscribed to the Author of the Farce by HD, 1764. The Library Company of Philadelphia.

to the capital city to protect the Indians who remained there. Franklin, no doubt wanting to discredit the Penns, painted a much different and self-serving story.[22] As the Paxton Boys approached Philadelphia, Franklin told a friend, "this Proprietary Governor did me the Honour, on an Alarm, to run to my House at Midnight, with his Counsellors at his Heels, for Advice." Together, Franklin and Penn rode to the edge of town to meet the Paxton Boys, who, seeing that Philadelphia was not inhabited solely by Quakers who would turn the other cheek, agreed to leave. In just twenty-four hours, Franklin wryly observed, he "was a common Soldier, a Counsellor, a kind of Dictator, an Ambassador to the Country Mob, and on their Returning home, Nobody."[23]

Of course Benjamin Franklin had no intention of being a "nobody." His hostility to the Proprietors may well have abated had John Penn treated him with the respect that he thought his heroics deserved. Instead, Penn berated the assembly for its reluctance to support military efforts to maintain order on the frontier. When the governor vetoed a spending bill that taxed the Proprietary estates along with a new militia bill—claiming that both technically defied his uncles' instructions—Franklin's personal hostility to the Penns bubbled to the surface once more. Insisting that Pennsylvania had been treated shabbily by the Proprietors one too many times, he determined to have his revenge. Thus he began his ill-fated and embarrassing campaign for royal government in earnest.

Franklin assured Richard Jackson, Pennsylvania agent and Member of Parliament, that the Proprietary government was "universally dislik'd" in the colony.[24] Most inhabitants of the province may indeed have been unhappy with the Penns for one reason or another, but this did not mean that they thought a Crown takeover would solve their problems. Nor were they wrong to be leery of the project. Granted, Franklin had his enemies in Pennsylvania, men who would oppose virtually anything he proposed. But there were many others who bore him no animus and still had good reason to fear Crown rule. The most important opposition came from religious minorities. Presbyterians and Moravians, in particular, valued the religious liberty that was at the very heart of Pennsylvania's identity and could not help wondering if their cherished liberty would be ignored or even destroyed if the colony's charter were abolished. Even some Quakers looked askance at Franklin's plan. Would an Anglican king give them the protection they had always enjoyed? Would he even endorse William Penn's guarantee of religious liberty? And how would the position of the assembly be improved if lawmakers had to answer to the king rather than to the Proprietors? King George III was an unknown quantity. He might well become an enemy to the liberties of the colony. And even if George was benevolent, who knew what might happen under his successors?

Neither Franklin nor Joseph Galloway, his most dedicated partner in the campaign for royal government, could answer these hypothetical questions to the satisfaction of their opponents. Franklin in particular had been warned by his English friends that royal government might actually be worse than anything Pennsylvania had faced under the Penns. They also pointed out that neither the king nor his advisers was likely to look kindly on any popular efforts to destroy a legitimate government. But Franklin would not be dissuaded. To a large extent, he was in the grip of his own raw emotions. Historians too often take Franklin at his word, believing his portrayal of himself as a man without passion who avoided arguments at almost any cost. In fact, while he may have been slow to anger, once his ire was aroused he found it difficult if not impossible to forgive and forget. His personal hatred of the Penns clearly played an essential role in his determination to destroy the Proprietors.

And so the campaign for royal government began. Galloway used his oratorical gifts to whip up support for the project, while Franklin employed his own literary skills to his advantage. His *Cool Thoughts on the Present Situation of Public Affairs* was a lucid—if not always persuasive—attack on Proprietary government. Not only were the Penns selfish and avaricious, he argued, but they were not very effective governors. John Penn's inability to control the Paxton Boys without Franklin's help simply proved his point. Indeed, Franklin predicted, there would be "little internal Quiet in the Administration of our Publick Affairs" until the Proprietors were removed.[25]

Franklin also tried to reassure those who worried that the loss of their charter would lead to the loss of their liberties. Unable to imagine a time when the interests of the colonies and England would be at odds, he was convinced that Pennsylvanians had nothing to fear from Crown rule. To the contrary, he confidently insisted, the colony would be much safer if it were governed by "a gracious King" instead of by "self-interested Proprietaries." The king would always "be at Liberty to join with the Assembly in enacting wholesome Laws," something that the rigid and unbending Penns would never do.[26] At a minimum, the king owned no private land in the colony and hence had no pecuniary interest separate from and in opposition to the welfare of the province. Simply put, the king was public-spirited; the Proprietors thought only in terms of their own pocketbooks.

Franklin clearly misjudged Pennsylvania's political climate. He and Galloway found the going much tougher than they had expected. They launched a petition campaign designed to prove that most Pennsylvanians wanted a change of government, but their efforts to gain signatures fell flat. Even more troubling, many Quakers—including Isaac Norris—opposed the plan. Norris was so unhappy with the aims of his own party that he resigned as Speaker. Undaunted, Franklin eagerly sought and easily won election to Norris's post. When he used his new position to persuade the assembly to send a petition for royal government to England, he was elated. But not for long.

Franklin's opponents, led by a hitherto unknown Presbyterian, John Dickinson, decided to turn the election of 1764 into a referendum on royal government. Franklin and Galloway had organization and experience on their side. But the opposition was unfazed. What it lacked in skill it more than made up for in its ability to mount an emotional propaganda campaign against key members of the Quaker Party. The run-up to the election was, even by Pennsylvania standards, a nasty one. Franklin bore the brunt of the personal onslaught. He was, his opponents reminded the voters, the father of a bastard child. He was a canny politician who stood to gain personally from a change in government. In fact, whispered some, his real aim was to become Pennsylvania's first royal governor. He had already managed to help his son, William, secure the governorship of neighboring New Jersey. No doubt he had a Franklin dynasty in his sights. Clearly his personal aspirations knew no bounds. They also pointed out that Franklin had once maligned the integrity of the very German inhabitants whose votes had always been part of the Quaker Party's winning coalition. Why should Germans support a man who so obviously disdained them? There were even rumors that Franklin's famed kite experiment was a fraud, based on the findings of other scientists.

Franklin struggled mightily to diminish the effects of the slanderous attacks and reasoned arguments that he and his plan endured. His efforts were not enough. The Quaker Party suffered heavy losses in the October election. Franklin and Galloway were turned out of office as were many of their allies. A pragmatic man would have recognized the obvious, admitting that his goals were not shared by most Pennsylvanians. But Franklin easily rationalized his defeat, deciding that it was due to the "scurrilous Pamphlets" and the "personal Abuse" hurled at him by his opponents.[27] It had nothing to do with the merits of his plan. Fortunately for him—at least in the short run—the Quaker Party managed to hang on to a slim majority of seats in the assembly. Thus, bowing to the pressure that the party's erstwhile leaders exerted from behind the scenes, the lower house refused to retract its petition for royal government. Instead, ignoring the strong objections of Dickinson's supporters, it voted to send Benjamin Franklin back to London in order to secure the Privy Council's positive response to the petition.

Even before the results of the election were in, Franklin was looking forward to a possible return to England. If he lost, he promised William Strahan, "Behold me a Londoner for the rest of my Days." He had been "the Butt of Party Rage and Malice" for much too long, and he was understandably eager to put all the factional acrimony and vicious attacks on his character behind him.[28] His timing, however, could not have been worse. George Grenville had come to his office of chief minister in July 1763 with a plan. England was suffering under a deep postwar recession; its inhabitants were already taxed to the limit and beyond. Moreover, at a time when prolonged deficit spending was not viewed as an option, the government was deeply in debt—to the tune of over 133 million pounds. It was Grenville's task to get rid of all that red ink, and he eagerly embraced the challenge. To lighten the financial burden on English taxpayers, he wanted the colonies to contribute at least a fraction of the cost of maintaining those British soldiers who remained in America at the end of the French and Indian War. Thus the Grenville administration introduced legislation that taxed the colonies. The Sugar Act—or, as some colonists called it, the Revenue Act—of 1764 cut in half the old duty on foreign (primarily French) sugar and molasses that entered American harbors. But while the former duty had been intended to discourage colonial commerce with the French altogether, and hence was essentially a constitutional effort to regulate trade, the new one was intended to raise money. It was, in other words, a tax.

The Sugar Act would do the most damage in New England. Its practical effect would be minimal elsewhere. The Stamp Act, however, destined to go into effect on November 1, 1765, inflamed colonists from one end of the continent to the other. It would levy taxes on a wide array of paper items, including court documents, newspapers, merchant papers, and playing cards. Each item would have a stamp affixed to it, proof that the purchaser had paid the required—generally very small—tax. To make his proposal more palatable, Grenville decided to pay certain lucky colonists to distribute the stamped paper. Thus no one could complain that swarms of greedy outsiders were profiting from Parliament's bill.

Not surprisingly, Pennsylvania' opponents of royal government seized upon both the Sugar Act and the Stamp Act as evidence that trust in the goodwill of the Crown was more dangerous than reliance on the benevolence of the Proprietors. In September 1764, just as the election campaign went into the final stretch, the Pennsylvania Assembly discussed the impending legislation. Constitutional principles, not economic concerns, dominated the debate. In the end the lower house instructed agent Richard Jackson to oppose Grenville's program, fearing that it would "have a Tendency to deprive the good People of this Province of their most essential Rights as British Subjects." All Englishmen, they said, had "the Right of assessing their own Taxes, and of being free from any Impositions but those that are made by their own Representatives."[29] As Speaker of the House, Benjamin Franklin signed the instructions. But he seemed curiously undisturbed by the implications of Grenville's proposals.

Before he left for England, Franklin brought the matter up in a private letter to Richard Jackson. He did not so much as mention the constitutional principles that troubled so many colonists. He no doubt agreed that Parliament's taxes violated the rights of Englishmen. But he thought that bringing issues of "rights" to the forefront of the debate would just stir up a hornet's nest, angering members of Parliament who would not take kindly to moralistic lectures from lowly colonists. To the contrary, Franklin actually pointed to a number of other items, goods that he designated as luxuries, which the government might want to tax. "A Duty not only on Tea, but on all East India Goods," he casually suggested, "might perhaps not be amiss."[30]

Once in London, Franklin remained unconcerned. Having arrived just as Grenville was preparing to submit the Stamp Act to Parliament, he—with the other agents—was in a position to launch a protest. He did so, but in a perfunctory sort of way, and when Grenville ignored his feeble objections, he shrugged. Writing to a friend, he remarked, "Depend upon it my good Neighbour, I took every Step in my Power, to prevent the Passing of the Stamp Act." Unfortunately, he added, "We might as well have hinder'd the Suns setting. That we could not do. But since 'tis down, my Friend, and it may be long before it rises again, Let us make as good a Night of it as we can."[31]

Wedderburn's wild "incendiary" was so unconcerned by the issues that disturbed many colonists that he secured the position of Stamp Distributor in Philadelphia for his friend, John Hughes. He also purchased reams of inexpensive stamped paper to send to his partners in Philadelphia and elsewhere, hoping to spare them some of the cost of the tax. Saving money, not defending colonial rights, seemed to be his uppermost concern.

Even Franklin's friends were puzzled by his attitude. There are a number of explanations for Franklin's initially cavalier response to Grenville's legislation. In part, he honestly believed that neither the Sugar Act nor the Stamp Act posed an especially grave threat. A comment he made to Richard Jackson is illuminating. "If," he said, "you lay such Duties as may destroy our Trade with the Foreign Colonies, I think you will greatly hurt your own Interest as well as ours."[32] In essence, Franklin was a reasonable man who assumed that most people were as rational and as aware of their own self-interest as he was. He firmly believed that if England's taxes and trade regulations became so oppressive that they threatened to destroy the colonial economy, England would also suffer. Impoverished colonists, after all, would not be able to purchase many of the manufactured goods that English merchants sent their way. Thus London would soon come to its senses, repealing any legislation that threatened the economic health of its American possessions.

That being the case, England needed to be reminded in the clearest way possible just how important colonial consumers really were. Thus one of Franklin's favorite ploys was to advise Americans to be thriftier, to avoid spending money on luxuries, and to boycott all English goods. When merchants throughout the colonies vowed to import nothing from England so long as the Stamp Act remained in effect, Franklin was delighted. Nonimportation was legal; it did not lead to riots; and it would give Englishmen solid evidence of just how much they depended on colonial trade. He simply ignored the argument of his friend, Charles Thomson, who pointed out with some asperity that the more the colonists saved, the richer they would be, and the more tempting it would be for England to tax its possessions at ever-higher levels.[33]

But Franklin had more self-interested reasons for keeping a low profile in the early stages of the Stamp Act controversy. He was, for starters, a royal officeholder who owed his very position to George III. He was proud of his status as deputy postmaster, enjoyed the revenue his sinecure brought, and hoped to earn more Crown preferments in the future. A frontal attack on Grenville's policies would be devastating to his prospects. More important, however, there was his campaign for royal government. How could he rail against the despotism of the king's ministers while he was trying to persuade the Privy Council to make Pennsylvania a Crown colony? And how would the Council respond to riots in Philadelphia? Wouldn't its members see such behavior as an indication that Franklin was wrong to insist that the vast majority of Pennsylvanians eagerly anticipated a Crown takeover? Ultimately, his obsession with ousting the Penns completely blinded Franklin to political reality. As a result, the Stamp Act crisis came perilously close to destroying his political career. A decade later, he still found it necessary to explain that he had never approved Grenville's legislation, an indication of just how serious a blunder his initial reaction to the Stamp Act was.[34]

As Franklin saw it at the time, his plan for royal government depended upon putting his colony in the best possible light. That required Pennsylvanians to stifle their impulse to protest the Stamp Act; to the contrary, they had to obey the act when it went into effect. He urged the Quaker Party to do all it could to secure compliance, if not support, for the offensive legislation. He instructed David Hall, his partner and the editor of the *Pennsylvania Gazette*, not to use his paper to attack the Stamp Act. And when Hall reported that his stance had led to a drastic decline in readers—he estimated that some five hundred customers had canceled their subscriptions—Franklin told him not to waver.[35] Similarly, while he admitted to John Hughes that his friend's position as Stamp Distributor might make him "unpopular for a Time," he maintained that "a firm loyalty to the Crown, and faithful Adherence to the Government of the Nation, which it is the Safety as well as the Honour of the Colonies to be connected with, will always be the wisest Course for you and I to take."[36]

But the Proprietors and their supporters did not allow Franklin to have his way. They were determined to reap untold benefits from the turmoil surrounding the Stamp Act. While Franklin and Galloway were urging Pennsylvanians to do nothing to incur the wrath of the English government, the members of the Proprietary Party noted that when he first heard about it, Thomas Penn had lobbied vigorously against the legislation. Even as the assembly, dominated by Franklin's Quaker Party, virtually ignored the Stamp Act, the Proprietors' supporters led protests against the taxes, pointing out what should have seemed clear even to Franklin. A change of government was not something to be entertained lightly; Crown authority could not be trusted.

To say that Franklin was caught off guard by colonial reaction to the Stamp Act would be an understatement. He was finally shocked out of his lethargy when news of colonial riots filtered into London. Disavowing "all the riotous tumultuous opposition" to the Stamp Act, he was stunned when he learned of the devastation the Boston crowd had wreaked on the residence of his friend, Thomas Hutchinson.[37] He was appalled and even a little frightened as mob violence spread to other colonies as well. By the middle of September, the unrest finally threatened to spread to Philadelphia. Rumors had been circulating throughout the city for some time, indicating that "instead of doing anything to prevent" the Stamp Act from going into effect, Franklin had actually "helped to plan it when last in England."[38] Thus an antistamp mob was preparing to march on the residences of Stamp Distributor John Hughes and Franklin himself, doing to them what ruffians had already done elsewhere. William Franklin rushed to Philadelphia, begging both his sister and mother to return with him to the safety of the governor's mansion in Burlington. But while she finally agreed to send Sally to New Jersey, Deborah refused to budge. Instead, determined to protect her property from all comers, she boarded herself up in her house and, with the help of a few friends and relatives, promised to fire on anyone who tried to harm her. Luckily, Deborah's threats were not put to the test. Some eight hundred "sober Inhabitants" posted themselves throughout the town on the night in question, keeping everything "tolerably quiet."[39] Nevertheless, it had been a close call. Only the fact that Pennsylvania politics was so fractured made it possible to keep violence there at bay. Even so, the Proprietors' supporters could not help but point out the obvious irony of the situation. It was Franklin's Quaker Party that intervened to protect John Hughes and his ilk from certain attack. It was the Proprietors who appeared to be on the side of liberty.

It would take a very adroit politician to recover from the damage that Franklin had managed to do to his own reputation in so short a time. As it turned out, he was up to the task—and he was the beneficiary of more than a little luck as well. In July 1765, for reasons that had nothing to do with imperial affairs, George III demanded George Grenville's resignation. Simply put, the king "loathed" Grenville and was willing to trust his government to virtually anyone else.[40] Thus, a coalition government headed by the Marquis of Rockingham took Grenville's place. The Rockingham ministry was inexperienced, weak, and disunified, and in the beginning it had no particular desire to repeal the Stamp Act. Indeed, when news about the riots in Boston arrived in London, most members of Parliament—including many of Rockingham's men—talked, not about repeal, but about stepped-up efforts to enforce the law, using British troops if necessary. But as it became clear that no colonist would purchase so much as a single piece of stamped paper, Rockingham began looking for a dignified way out of the dilemma that his predecessor had left him. With a sympathetic ministry in power, Franklin could finally work for repeal without any fear of damaging his relationship with the king's men.

He swung quickly into action. Although it galled him to have to do so, he insisted in no uncertain terms that he had nothing to do with the framing of the Stamp Act. "It was all cut and dried, and every Resolve framed at the Treasury ready for the House, before I arrived in England," he assured his son. Thus rumors that Grenville had offered Franklin a sinecure as a reward for his support were preposterous.[41] To the contrary, he insisted that he was "extreamly busy, attending Members of both Houses, informing, explaining, consulting, disputing, in a continual Hurry from Morning to Night," doing everything he could to secure repeal of the Stamp Act.[42] Beginning in November, and reaching a crescendo by mid-January 1766, he inundated London newspapers with defenses of the colonies and attacks on the Stamp Act.

Always Franklin sought pragmatic ways out of the morass. He steadily urged Americans to couch their protests in "humble and dutiful Terms," insisting that violence would be "pernicious to America in general."[43] When he visited Lord Dartmouth, who had recently been appointed head of the Board of Trade, he talked of tactics, not principles. He advised the government to return to the old requisition system. He also suggested a face-saving way out of the hole that Parliament had dug for itself. He thought the government might be wise simply to suspend the Stamp Act for a number of years. Then, he continued, it could quietly repeal the unpopular legislation "on some decent Pretence, without ever bringing the Question of Right to a Decision."

Finally, on January 14, 1766, Parliament convened, prepared at last to address the vexing problem of the Stamp Act. William Pitt, who had been absent from London due to debilitating illness, was the most eloquent spokesman for total repeal. By this time he had gone on record arguing that Parliament could legislate for the colonies but could not tax them. The Stamp Act, he insisted, was "unconstitutional, unjust, oppressive"; it was also "unnecessary."[44] Not surprisingly, Grenville was the act's most vociferous defender. He thought the claim that Parliament could legislate for but not tax the colonies was absurd. Taxation, he maintained, was simply a form of legislation. To limit Parliament's power in any respect was to deny its sovereignty, thus weakening the government, inviting further tumults, and leading irrevocably to American independence.

Almost a month to the day after debate over the Stamp Act had begun in the House of Commons, Franklin had his day in the sun. The House had called a number of witnesses—lawyers, merchants, colonists, and the like—to give the lawmakers their most considered advice. Benjamin Franklin—colonial agent, deputy postmaster, and self-described expert on colonial affairs—was the star witness on February 13. He knew ahead of time what the proponents of repeal would ask him. He had no idea what questions the opposition would pose. Nevertheless, he remained calm and confident throughout his testimony, parrying thrusts with wit and humor. Even so, while he was triumphant in the short run, some of his remarks had unintended consequences. Franklin was either too focused on the immediate problems facing England and its colonies to care about the long-term results of his testimony or he simply failed to understand the views of colonial leaders.

From a tactical perspective, Franklin's testimony was brilliant. He seldom lost his cool, patiently answering the same questions over and over again. He was particularly effective when he discussed the practical difficulties the Stamp Act posed. Distributing the stamps to the backcountry, for instance, where roads and urban centers were virtually nonexistent, would be difficult at best. He also reminded his audience that the colonists were still suffering from the effects of the Seven Years' War. No matter what skeptical critics said, they had contributed enormously, in men, supplies, and money, to the war effort. Thus, they were mired in debt and no more able to contribute to the government's coffers than their English counterparts were.

Franklin made two major points. First, he insisted that if England pushed too hard, the colonists were perfectly capable of taking care of their own material needs. This argument was aimed at English merchants who harbored fears of an economically self-sufficient America. Franklin knew that Grenville's supporters were convinced that, given time, the colonial boycott would collapse, as Americans became desperate for goods that only England could supply. Indeed, just two years earlier, Franklin had said much the same thing, categorically declaring that despite the jingoistic claims of some colonists, it would be "impossible" for Americans even to clothe themselves in the near future. "Our Sheep," he said then, "have such small Fleeces, that the Wool of all the Mutton we eat will not supply us with Stockings."[45] Now, however, he maintained that his countrymen were on the road to economic independence. "I do not know," he asserted, "a single article imported into the Northern Colonies, but what they can either do without, or make themselves." They could raise their own sheep, produce their own cloth, and develop manufacturing centers that would produce everything they needed.[46]

Franklin's second objective was one with which most Americans would be pleased. There was nothing, he repeatedly insisted, that would change colonial minds about the Stamp Act. Even if the government managed to make the act more economically palatable, the colonists would never pay taxes "unless compelled by force of arms."[47] If that happened, the Stamp Act would lead to the very destruction of the Empire that Englishmen were trying to avoid. Franklin maintained that up until the present controversy, virtually all Americans thought England was the "best [country] in the world."[48] While some narrow-minded Englishmen looked upon the colonies as "foreigners," the colonists saw themselves as "a part of the British empire, and as having one common interest with it."[49] Nor, until now, had anyone in America ever questioned Parliament's authority. To the contrary, like Englishmen everywhere the colonists "considered the parliament as the great bulwark and security of their liberties and privileges, and always spoke of it with the utmost respect and veneration."[50] Now, however, their loyalty was in jeopardy. If the Members of Parliament continued their ill-advised policy, he warned, "they will not find a rebellion; they may indeed make one."[51]

So far, so good. If they had been present during Franklin's testimony, most Americans would have applauded his performance. But if Franklin was firm and unequivocal in most ways, he invited serious trouble in others. To be sure, he struggled desperately to avoid any statement concerning Parliament's right to tax. Directly challenging that right would do more harm than good. Still, when pressed, he implied that the colonists believed that while Parliament could not levy "internal taxes" in America, they thought that "external taxes"— such as the tax on tea that he, himself had suggested less than two years earlier—were constitutional. They might, of course, object to the cost of an external tax, but they would never question the "right of laying it."[52] This assertion puzzled everyone. The colonists had said nothing like this in any of their petitions against the Stamp Act. Colony after colony had railed against "taxation without representation"; not one had made the distinction that Franklin was now making with such apparent confidence. Again and again the men who sat before him asked their witness to clarify his position, trying to make sure that what they heard was what Franklin actually meant to say. Again and again, Franklin repeated his argument. "An external tax," he explained, "is a duty laid on commodities imported." Merchants who paid the duty would pass the cost on to the consumer, who, if he found the price too steep, would simply refuse to buy the commodity. "An internal tax," however, was "forced from the people without their consent."

In the case of the Stamp Act, a refusal to pay the tax would mean that commerce would grind to a halt and no one would be able to use the courts, make their wills, or even get married. It would, in other words "ruin" anyone who refused to pay it.[53] Franklin made the same case two years later, even after the Townshend Duties had become a bone of contention between England and the colonies.[54] For most members of Parliament, and for most Americans, Franklin was making a distinction without a difference. It was, moreover, a distinction that would come back to haunt him.

Still, the colonists scored an immediate victory. Eleven days after his testimony, Franklin reported that Parliament had begun to discuss the merits of repealing the Stamp Act. Although they were in the minority, Grenville's supporters fought a desperate rearguard action against repeal, and so on more than one occasion the highly emotional debate dragged on into the wee hours of the morning. It would take until the middle of March before repeal was a reality, but Franklin was confident from the beginning that Rockingham would prevail. Determined to remain on the good side of the new ministry, he gave generous credit for this happy turn of events to the administration and its allies. Nor did he want those Englishmen who had exhibited the political courage to come to America's rescue to be embarrassed by the behavior of a few rash and intemperate colonials. Thus he begged for an end of "all Mobs and Riots on our Side the Water."[55]

Franklin had landed on his feet. His friends all agreed that his testimony was a triumph. He went from goat to hero overnight. Nothing he had done or said up until that time was as useful in discrediting the rumors about his apostasy as his testimony against the Stamp Act. There were those, of course, who continued to insist that Franklin was "the greatest Enemy to the Repeal of the Stamp Act, of all the Men in England."[56] Thomas Penn—more judiciously and more accurately— simply pointed out that Franklin had in reality done very little to secure the repeal and that his testimony had not tipped the balance. But most of his detractors found it difficult, in the face of Franklin's effective propaganda campaign, to do anything but maintain a sullen silence. Colonial newspapers eagerly published accounts of Franklin's appearance before the House. His London friends inundated Pennsylvania with accounts of Franklin's heroics. William Strahan was only one of many to insist, with considerable hyperbole, that "To this very

Examination, more than to any thing else, you are indebted to the speedy and total Repeal of this odious Law." Strahan fervently hoped that his friend's testimony was such unequivocal "proof of his Patriotism" that it would "forever silence his Enemies with you."[57] Not surprisingly, Franklin's Philadelphia admirers were almost giddy with relief. "Malice itself," crowed one, "is almost struck dumb."[58]

Franklin had salvaged his own reputation in Pennsylvania, and—wrongly as it turned out—assumed that all was right with the Empire. "We now see," he asserted confidently, "that tho' the Parliament may sometimes possibly thro' Misinformation be mislead to do a wrong Thing towards America, yet as soon as they are rightly inform'd, they will immediately rectify it."[59] Just who the source of that "misinformation" might have been, he did not say. He did not yet suspect Thomas Hutchinson of such perfidy, but he did think that it may have come from the Proprietors or their colonial lackeys.

In the meantime, he saw no cloud on the horizon. Even the Declaratory Act did not disturb him. He had managed quite nicely. Parliament had claimed that it had a right to legislate "in all cases whatsoever," but it had dropped any specific right to tax the colonies from its claims, and thus Americans might assume that it merely stated the obvious. True, many in Parliament believed that the Declaratory Act indicated that while England may have backed down on this single occasion, it had not retreated an inch from the principle that Parliament had a right to tax the colonies. But the language was fuzzy enough to be open to interpretation. Franklin tended to minimize the significance of the Declaratory Act. In his testimony before the House, he had signaled that parliamentary "resolutions of right" would not bother most colonists, so long as they were "never attempted to be carried into practice."[60] And he assured everyone that "this is merely to save Appearances, and to guard against the Effects of the Clamour made by the late Ministry." He was confident that "no future Ministry will ever attempt to tax us."[61]

For Franklin, there was only one fly in the ointment. His cherished plan for a change of government was not proceeding nearly as quickly as he had thought that it would. In November 1765 the Privy Council had finally agreed to hold hearings on the Pennsylvania Assembly's petition. But it came to no conclusion, postponing any actual discussion of the matter. Franklin did not know it then, but this would be the last time the government would even consider his project. In fact, he still refused to admit even the possibility of defeat. He thought that all the political winds were blowing in his direction. Grenville was gone. He had developed an excellent rapport with Rockingham. "If the present Ministry should be confirmed," he said, "as I sincerely pray they may, I hope another Winter will bring our Affairs all to a happy Conclusion."[62] His Quaker Party had proved its loyalty during the Stamp Act crisis and was heeding his advice, celebrating repeal with "great Prudence."[63] So long as the colonists did not directly challenge Parliament's power, the Privy Council would eventually come around.

Of course Franklin was wrong on most counts. The Rockingham administration fell victim to its own internal bickering and was out of power by the summer of 1766. William Pitt, now the Earl of Chatham, took Rockingham's place, but he was often ill and ceded much of the day-to-day direction of events to the Duke of Grafton and to Charles Townshend, the Chancellor of the Exchequer (the minister who oversaw all economic and financial matters). The mercurial Townshend took full advantage of the confusion that was the hallmark of the Chatham administration. He came to office determined both to relieve England from its mountain of debt and to force the colonies to acknowledge Parliament's authority. He was convinced, with good reason, that the colonists would accept an external tax, no matter what the petitions and pamphlets that emanated from colonial malcontents during the Stamp Act crisis had indicated. He knew that in fact—if not in principle—the colonists were willing to pay the very duties that a loud minority in America characterized as taxes. At the same time it repealed the Stamp Act, Parliament had quietly amended the Sugar Act, lowering the duty from three pence to one pence per gallon of sugar or molasses, and even in Boston merchants paid the new duty, choosing to see it as a regulation rather than a tax. Thus Franklin's testimony before the House had merely confirmed what Townshend already believed was the case. He admitted that he personally saw no difference between external and internal taxes. But if the colonists would accept the constitutionality of external taxes—and Franklin had assured everyone that this was the case—who was he to tell them that they were wrong?

Thus in June 1767 the Chancellor of the Exchequer proposed legislation that became known collectively as the Townshend Acts. The acts placed duties on certain designated luxury items—lead, paint, paper, glass, and tea—arriving in the colonies from England. To stop the smuggling of untaxed items into American ports, Parliament also created a Board of Customs Commissioners, headquartered in Boston, which would oversee a larger and more zealous band of customs collectors than had existed in the past. Townshend's aims were more ambitious—and more offensive—than Grenville's had been. The revenue he collected would go in part to pay the salaries of royal officials—governors and judges primarily—thus making the king's men independent of the elected colonial assemblies. Benjamin Franklin was wrong. The Declaratory Act was not just a face-saving measure. The Townshend Acts both legislated for and taxed the colonies. Clearly, Parliament had not retreated from its determination to uphold its sovereignty.

No matter what Benjamin Franklin had said in his testimony, colonial leaders did not distinguish—at least in principle—between external and internal taxation. To them, a tax was a tax, and all parliamentary taxation of the colonies was unconstitutional. Thus they geared up for action once more. They forwarded petitions to their agents, who were expected to guide their pleas through the intricate maze that constituted government bureaucracy. When that failed, they eventually fell back on what appeared to be a tried-and-true tactic, instituting nonimportation agreements that would go into effect in 1769. Economic pressure had worked before, they thought; perhaps it would work again. Knowing that during the Stamp Act crisis some demonstrations had gotten out of control, provincial leaders did not encourage crowd action. In some places, however, especially in Massachusetts, rioters occasionally took matters into their own hands.

Somewhat strangely, Franklin did not seem to be as alarmed by this new effort at taxation without representation as many of his compatriots were. He was still focused on his plan for royal government and was determined to do nothing to destroy what little chance for success remained. Moreover, he knew full well that he had put himself in an awkward position. There was his testimony before the House of Commons to explain. And just three months before the Townshend Acts became law, Franklin had publicly reiterated his stance, maintaining that "the colonies submit to pay all external taxes laid on them by way of duty on merchandizes imported into their country, and never disputed the authority of parliament to lay such duties."[64] Consequently, while plenty of letters from the Pennsylvania Assembly instructed him and Richard Jackson to make every effort to get the Townshend Acts repealed, Jackson worked harder on the issue than Franklin did. Franklin's private letters seldom mentioned the Townshend Duties. True, he supported nonimportation, but he seemed more invested in urging Americans to avoid attacks on persons or property than he was in advocating resistance to external taxation.

Admittedly, Franklin did try to explain the American perspective on the Townshend Acts to the English public. In January 1768, he submitted an essay to the *London Chronicle* to that effect. "Causes of the American Discontents before 1768" explained that, rightly or wrongly (Franklin did not say which), all Americans believed that parliamentary taxation of the colonies was unconstitutional. It also defended the nonimportation agreements. Most of his articles against the Townshend Acts, however, advanced practical arguments, carefully avoiding discussion of parliamentary rights.[65] It actually fell to another Pennsylvanian, the leading opponent of Franklin's plan for a change of government, to launch the most effective constitutional attack on the Townshend Acts. John Dickinson's *Letters from a Farmer in Pennsylvania to the Inhabitants of the British Colonies* began appearing in Pennsylvania in December 1767. Essentially, Dickinson made clear what many of the colonies had been trying to say all along. Until 1764, Parliament had regulated colonial trade, occasionally levying duties on American imports, but never taxing the colonies. Thus any effort to tax them now was an unwelcome and unconstitutional innovation. If Benjamin Franklin had distinguished between internal and external taxes, Dickinson drew the line between Parliament's authority over trade and its power to tax.

Privately, Franklin was moving to a position that—for once—was ahead of the curve rather than behind it. Even before he knew who wrote them, he made sure that the *Farmer's Letters* were published in London. But after he read Dickinson's essays he admitted to his son that he was not sure Dickinson's construction worked any better than his own had done. This, too, might be a distinction without a difference. It was, he mused, "difficult to draw lines between duties for regulation and those for revenue." And if Parliament could interpret the purposes of its own legislation, simply deciding to its own satisfaction that something was a regulation rather than a tax, then for all practical purposes it could do pretty much as it pleased. Franklin was becoming convinced that there was "no middle ground." Either, as the Declaratory Act maintained, Parliament enjoyed complete legislative power over the colonies, or it had none at all. The more he considered the matter, the more he thought that the latter interpretation was the most logical. But this was not an argument that he was prepared to advance in public.[66] Instead he continued to press for royal government in Pennsylvania and to do his best to tamp down the rhetoric of advocates on both sides of the water.

It was not until 1770 that Franklin began to be seen as a real thorn in the side of the English establishment. Although he continued to believe that men like Burke or Rockingham would somehow regain control of Parliament, he nevertheless recognized that so long as hardliners remained in power, he could expect little change. When Lord North became chief minister at the beginning of 1770, Franklin temporarily hoped that the new administration would be sympathetic to American concerns. Instead, a variety of circumstances led him to the conclusion that only a firm defense of colonial rights would lead Parliament to change its course. By 1770, even he had to admit that his plan for a change of government in Pennsylvania was dead. And, given the direction in which British policy seemed to be moving, he was finally willing to concede that this was just as well.

Nothing moved Franklin to a more critical position on English policy than the decision of the Massachusetts Assembly to appoint him as its agent. Without question, the Bay Colony was the most "radical" of His Majesty's mainland possessions. It had been the scene of more protests and more violence than any other province. Its relationship with Crown officials was also more vituperative than it was elsewhere. If Franklin were to represent so troublesome a colony, he would have to be more vigorous in his demands for the preservation of colonial rights. Aware that his appointment was unpopular in some circles, Franklin knew that if he was to keep his job, he would need to prove himself worthy of the colony's trust.

Franklin had the opportunity to begin earning that trust when, on March 5, 1770, Parliament voted to repeal most, but not all, of the

Townshend Duties. The House decided to keep the duty on tea because, Franklin noted acerbically, it continued to be infatuated with the "idle Notion of the Dignity and Sovereignty of Parliament."[67] Still, he thought that the colonies might win a complete victory if they stood firm. He was convinced that the colonial boycott had been responsible for the partial repeal of the Townshend Duties. Thus, it was reasonable to predict that "if our Merchants continue their Resolutions another Year," the tax on tea would also be abandoned.[68]

Unfortunately, the colonists were as disappointing in their own way as the North administration had been. Franklin pounded away at the need to keep the nonimportation policy alive. He knew that if Americans accepted a partial victory as good enough, and resumed trading with England, no one would ever again fear what looked like their idle threats. Parliament would assume that the colonists' desire for superior English goods would invariably outweigh their purported concerns about constitutional principle. And so he kept up a steady drumbeat, urging provincial leaders to "adhere firmly to our Agreements till the End for which they were entred into was fully obtained."[69] If Franklin was ever the "incendiary" that Wedderburn claimed that he was, this was his moment. But even then, the nonimportation movement in which Franklin put such stock aimed only at the repeal of the Townshend Duties and a return to the imperial relationship that had existed before 1763. Reform, not revolution, was his goal.

Still, after 1770, Benjamin Franklin became increasingly discouraged. While his loyalty to the king did not waver, his distrust of the king's ministers—especially Lord Hillsborough—became more pronounced. But even after Hillsborough resigned both as president of the Board of Trade and as secretary of state for the American Department, Franklin often found himself at odds with the powers that be. He corresponded much more with Boston leaders than he did with officials in the other provinces he represented. From Massachusetts he learned firsthand of the assembly's struggle to protect its liberties from the incursions of men like Thomas Hutchinson and Andrew Oliver. Moreover, it was his job to defend the Bay Colony's interests. As his visibility increased, and more and more people linked him with the Massachusetts Assembly, he became the focal point of those Englishmen who were looking for someone to blame for the problems that beset the Empire. Thus, although Franklin continued to search for ways to bridge the increasingly wide gap between England and the colonies, Wedderburn found it all too easy to brand him as the instigator of rebellion.

And so the question remains: What was Franklin thinking? Did he send the Hutchinson/Oliver letters across the Atlantic in order to ameliorate the differences between England and America? Or was he Wedderburn's "true incendiary," who was trying to push the colonies toward rebellion as early as 1773? At the very least, the solicitor's accusations do not seem likely.

Strange though it may seem, Franklin probably told the truth about his motives. He was, indeed, hoping to use the Hutchinson/Oliver letters to bring England and America closer together. His judgment had been wrong before, although with less drastic consequences. It might well have been wrong once more. He had noted on more than one occasion that "false advices" and "lying Letters said to be from Boston" were providing grist for the mill of Parliament's anti-American wing.[70] In his mind, his discovery of the Hutchinson/Oliver letters was simply proof of something he had suspected all along.

If anything, Franklin's fundamental error was the direct result of his emotional attachment to the Empire and of his naïve assumption that men more sympathetic to the colonies might yet rise to positions of power in England. While he became increasingly disenchanted with the corruption and ignorance that he believed characterized English politics in the 1770s, almost until the end he held out hope that reconciliation was possible. He never understood that even America's most valiant supporters, men like Edmund Burke and the Earl of Chatham, could not accept his own or the colonists' conception of the Anglo-colonial relationship. They were no more willing to limit Parliament's claims to sovereignty than were Grenville's supporters. So convinced was Franklin of the ultimate goodwill of most Englishmen that he found it impossible to believe that any but a few bad apples meant the colonies any harm. If that were the case, only letters from selfish and mercenary Americans could explain the behavior of Parliament, the ministry, and eventually King George III himself.

Nor was Franklin the only one on either side of the Atlantic who was guilty of misjudgments in the years following the Seven Years' War. In the colonies, most observers continued to hope that a show of economic force, coupled with their own carefully reasoned arguments, would prevail. In England, America's staunchest allies did not seem to comprehend the depth of the colonies' determination to defend what they saw as their rights. They truly thought that if Parliament promised that it would never tax its provincial possessions again, even if it did not give up the right to do so, all would be well. King George III and the hardliners in Parliament were even more out of touch with reality. The king assured Thomas Hutchinson that the Coercive Acts were just the right medicine to frighten Massachusetts, and hence the other colonies, into submission. He was convinced that once Americans realized that England would no longer tolerate their disobedience, the slide toward "anarchy" would be halted once and for all.[71] Ironically, Thomas Hutchinson was one of the few individuals who recognized just how wide the gap between America and England had become. No one in England, he said, not Burke, not Chatham, not even rabble rouser John Wilkes, would ever stop defending the supremacy of Parliament. And virtually no American, if forced to choose between the "absolute authority" of Parliament and the "absolute Independency" of the colonies would hesitate to support the latter.[72] In the final analysis, Hutchinson was right. He watched in dismay as both sides decided to call one another's bluff, knowing full well that, by 1775, no one was bluffing.

CHAPTER 4

....

Dueling Conspiracies

When Alexander Wedderburn accused Benjamin Franklin of being the "prime conductor" of a cabal whose members sought to destroy the ties that bound England and its colonies together, he was not simply indulging in inflammatory rhetoric. His language may seem overheated, his message hyperbolic to modern ears, but Wedderburn knew that few of those present at the Cockpit would find his indictment particularly strange or hard to believe. Objectively speaking Franklin was no flame thrower. He had spent a decade in London trying, as he always put it, to explain the colonies to England and England to the colonies. In 1768 he wryly observed that he was the object of suspicion on both sides of the Atlantic due in large measure to his "impartiality." In England, he said, people thought he was "too much an American," while at home many saw him as "too much an Englishman."[1] Could this man who sought so valiantly and so long to "palliate matters" dividing the Empire be the "great incendiary" against whom Wedderburn railed with such conviction?[2]

The answer for most of those at the Cockpit was a resounding "yes." The solicitor general knew his audience. He was fully aware of the anxieties about colonial intentions that dominated the discourse in Whitehall and beyond in the years leading up to the Revolution. For at least a half-century prior to Benjamin Franklin's ordeal at the Cockpit, the Anglo-American political world was, in the words of one historian, virtually consumed by "an escalating mutuality of conspiratorial fears," and the men who applauded Wedderburn shared those fears.[3] So, too, did the few observers who condemned him. Ironically, Benjamin Franklin was one of a handful of individuals at the Cockpit who had generally resisted the conspiratorial language that so pervaded political rhetoric in England and America. It was his appearance before the Privy Council that led him, at long last, to embrace the view of England that many of his own compatriots had held for years. And it was that same appearance that led many Englishmen to the conclusion not only that they had been right to believe that the colonies were moving rapidly toward independence but also that Benjamin Franklin was largely responsible for the coming debacle.

It had been the case in less secular times that people tended to seek explanations for the troubles that often roiled the body politic in the realm of the supernatural. Some turned to "the gods," providence, or perhaps some hazy sense of fate to make sense of the vicissitudes that befell humankind on occasion. Others simply shrugged, taking it for granted that any government's failures were the inevitable consequence of original sin. Evil people, no matter how hard they strove to do otherwise, no matter how valiantly governments struggled to stop them, would by definition be unable to contain their passions or curb their destructive behavior. In an "enlightened" era, however, philosophers believed that governments were devised by rational men who could create a political structure that would reflect the universal laws of nature, thus ensuring the continuing stability of the body politic. Success—or failure—then was in the hands of ordinary human beings who either obeyed or ignored nature's immutable requirements. If, as seemed to be the case in England, there was no reason to tinker with the structure of the government itself, then observers drew the obvious conclusion: Something was clearly wrong and someone, somewhere, was to blame. The more difficult it was to figure out who was responsible for political disasters, the more certain people became that a secret cabal was behind the demise of a once-functioning polity.

Nowhere was this penchant for seeing conspiracies behind every rock and tree more prevalent than in eighteenth-century Britain. Ironically, the sense of vulnerability experienced by so many in both England and America had its roots in the very characteristics that led most political theorists to see the British government as a model of wisdom and virtue. At least since the end of the Glorious Revolution, the British enjoyed what contemporaries—echoing Aristotle's ideal—characterized as a "mixed government." Comprised of the monarchy (the king and his ministers), the nobility (the House of Lords), and the rest of the king's subjects (the House of Commons), it represented and presumably protected the interests of everyone in the Empire. Such a government depended for its success on "balance." So long as everyone had a voice and no one intruded upon the rights and privileges of any other, it was about as perfect a structure as humans could create, for it could steer successfully between the equally undesirable extremes of tyranny and anarchy. But should the king or his men interfere with the House of Commons, for instance, "corrupting" its members with offers of money or position, then tyranny would result. If—less likely, but still possible—the balance tipped too far toward the Commons, then the consequence was anarchy.

A balanced government may have been essential, but it was almost impossible to sustain. Government (and by this most people in England meant the king and his ministers) was, by its very nature, avaricious and power-hungry. Monarchs, in particular, could not help but seek to augment their own power at the expense of the people's liberty. If they could not achieve their ends openly, they did so by subterfuge. Unfortunately, because power was aggressive and manipulative, it tended to have its way. It was "like a cancer," eating "faster and faster every hour" until it had utterly demolished its prey.[4] It was up to "the people," whose interests were protected in the Commons, to defend weak and passive liberty as best they could. Throughout the eighteenth century, Englishmen on both sides of the Atlantic were horrified whenever they observed the ease and regularity with which tyrannical rulers destroyed liberty in all parts of the globe. Many colonists saw the situation as grim indeed, convinced that they, alone, had the ability to contain the abuse of power.

By the middle of the eighteenth century, many English leaders had become less concerned about the rise of tyranny and more fearful that in the mainland colonies the balance had tipped too far toward what they referred to as the "democratical" part of government. King George III himself pushed his ministers to exhibit "firmness and resolution" whenever they dealt with Americans, arguing that "this alone can restore order and save this country from anarchy." He refused to see colonial protests as legitimate expressions of anger directed at specific grievances, convinced that riots gave every "appearance of a plan" devised by rapacious malcontents.[5] Supremely confident of their own good intentions, sure that their measures to gain a modicum of control over the colonies were fair, reasonable, and did no violence to the precepts upon which England's unwritten constitution rested, the king and his advisers were genuinely bewildered by America's resistance to their efforts to gain a small and much needed revenue from the colonies. When provincial orators accused them of tyranny and worse, they were disbelieving. Had not enlightened French philosophers such as Voltaire and Montesquieu proclaimed that they envied the British system, seeing it as an almost perfect mixture of monarchical stability and republican liberty? Were the king's subjects wrong to boast of Parliament's dedication to the preservation of the "rights of Englishmen," rights that had been hard won as a result of the Glorious Revolution of 1688?

Seeing their rule as the most tolerant and beneficent in human history, Englishmen struggled to explain such obvious distortions of reality. There was, as they saw it, only one plausible explanation for the unrest. In every colony there existed a small but very able and determined group of demagogues whose numbers were seeking to sever the ties that bound England and America. They did so, not because English leaders had done anything wrong, but because they craved power for themselves. They seized upon any pretext, however flimsy, to stir up trouble, to convince unwitting colonists that the English government was up to its neck in a conspiracy designed to destroy their liberty. The more Americans protested their loyalty to England and their love of its monarch, the more English observers were convinced of the colonists' duplicitous ways. By 1774, nothing short of America's complete acceptance of Parliament's authority—especially when it involved the raising of revenue—would convince English politicians that provincial protesters were being truthful when they claimed that independence was not, and never had been, their goal.

Worried Englishmen believed they had ample evidence to support their suspicions. Especially after mid-century, they received a stream of reports from reputable eyewitnesses who warned them that a few influential colonists were determined to obtain independence.

Thomas Hutchinson and Andrew Oliver were by no means the king's only loyal subjects who begged Parliament to gain control of the situation before it was too late. Complaints began in earnest during the Seven Years' War. Both John Campbell, Earl of Loudoun, commander of the king's forces in mainland America, and his successor, Sir Jeffrey Amherst, inundated the ministry with accounts of colonial foot-dragging and even disloyalty. They railed at smugglers in New England who continued to trade with the French enemy at the very time that stalwart English soldiers risked their lives to protect the colonies from a Canadian invasion. They bemoaned the reluctance of local assemblies to raise the money, men, and supplies the king's forces needed in order to prosecute the war. Loudoun, in particular, was convinced of the existence of a full-blown conspiracy headed by Massachusetts governor William Shirley, who, he said had "designs" to create a republican army that would destroy the order and discipline that was essential to the success of a respectable military force.[6]

Even at war's end when England was finally able to relish its victory over the French, military leaders continued to send messages home describing the "dangerous designs" that the colonies' "popular leaders" harbored.[7] General Thomas Gage considered himself a friend of America. But after 1767, especially when he discussed the colony of Massachusetts, he could not restrain himself, convinced that the ordinary people of Boston were innocent victims, "led astray" and "nourished" by the "Seditious Spirit" of malcontents such as Samuel Adams and John Hancock.[8]

Colonial governors also wrote home, sometimes in anger, increasingly in fear, describing their precarious position. From their perspective, government in the colonies was unbalanced; the elected assemblies were taking matters into their own hands, threatening to destroy all order. "The Popular Scale," cried Massachusetts governor Francis Bernard, "is so much weightier than the Royal," and thus his own position was "contemptibly weak." Nor was he alone. Crown officers throughout the colonies felt "defenceless," helpless to protect themselves from the rampaging mob.[9] More and more often the most conciliatory governors talked of the insidious motives and the "Sham Patriotism" of popular leaders.[10] Governor William Franklin, Benjamin's own son, assured Lord Dartmouth that even in the relatively moderate colony of New Jersey there were those who had a secret plan to "establish a

Republic." William never stopped believing that there were "Thousands" of Americans who longed to maintain their "Connexion with Great Britain" but who had been led astray by a few devious men.[11]

As tensions between England and America escalated, voices from the king's supporters in the colonies became shriller. Not able to admit that ordinary men and women truly feared and opposed parliamentary taxation, royal officeholders were sure that a "few crafty seditious popular malignants" had managed to dupe the "stupid herd of voters" who were being unwittingly stampeded into a movement for independence that none wanted. Rioters, they always said, were "egged on" by "Demagogues" who bribed them with liquor and—oddly enough— Cheshire cheese, leading them to acts of wanton destruction that they would never have conceived of on their own.[12] How else could anyone explain the utter destruction of Thomas Hutchinson's house and possessions in 1765? Was there any other way to account for the attacks in Boston and elsewhere on customs officials who were simply doing their jobs when they tried to collect duties on designated imports?

Not surprisingly, the men who described the move toward independence did not simply complain about their situation. Many, just as Hutchinson and Oliver had done, offered concrete suggestions for reform before it was too late. Governors, in particular, tirelessly provided evidence to prove that they were powerless to protect themselves against subversive elements in their own assemblies. All of them were convinced that those governors who did not enjoy an independent salary should have one, thus giving them at least a chance to fend off lawmakers who used the power of the purse to bend governors to their will. Some, like Francis Bernard, had a more ambitious agenda. Bernard repeatedly urged his superiors to grant the colonies representation in Parliament, not, he hastily explained, because they deserved it but because doing so would take the wind out of the radicals' sails. If Americans insisted that they could not be taxed without representation, he said, then "take them at their Word." Give them representatives—and then tax them.[13]

Everyone, those with specific policies in mind and those who had nothing to share but their frustrations, begged government officials to stand firm in the face of colonial protests. Whenever Parliament repealed legislation because it led to riots and boycotts, royal officials in America were demoralized. Bernard feared that if Parliament did nothing to shore up its authority, the colonies would "soon become an anarchical Democracy." As early as 1769 he was arguing that there was "but one Way now of dealing with America: Lenitives have brought the Disease to its present Height & will if continued make it incurable."[14] In what became his constant refrain, General Gage, too, insisted that "the Colonists are taking large strides toward Independency; and that it concerns Great Britain by a speedy and spirited Conduct to shew them that these provinces are British Colonies dependent on her, and that they are not independent States."[15] By 1768 Gage was desperate. "You can not Act," he cried, "with too much Vigour." The colonies viewed England's moderation as "Timidity," which ultimately led to "Sedition and Mutiny to a higher Pitch."[16] The Tea Party, as most observers at the Cockpit saw it, proved that those who had urged firmness for so long had been right. Parliament had given in too often and had earned nothing but the disdain of colonial dissidents in return. Assuming that indulgence had failed to stop the move toward independence, they hoped that a stern approach might, if it was not too late, do the trick. And if Benjamin Franklin was, indeed, the "prime mover" in a conspiracy that would lead to independence, then he and his cohorts in Boston must be punished.

It is hardly surprising that most observers at the Cockpit cheered when Alexander Wedderburn proclaimed that Benjamin Franklin was the instigator of a "conspiracy against the Governor" and hence against English authority. But Wedderburn and his admirers were by no means the only ones in the mid-eighteenth century to view events through the prism of conspiracy. Many colonists, too, saw sinister plots everywhere. They, however, were convinced that the king's ministers (although not the king himself) had launched a deliberate program to destroy liberty first in England and then in the colonies. They believed that the House of Commons, the very part of the government whose duty it was to protect liberty from avaricious power, had already lost its independence, succumbing to the bribes and threats of a powerful ministry. This alone could explain the willingness of Parliament—the very body designed to protect liberty—to pass laws that would turn the colonists into abject slaves. They had always known that this was a possibility, of course. But especially after 1763, many in America had begun to think that their once inchoate fears were rapidly being realized. It was essential, then, for all colonists to be on the lookout, not failing even for a moment to scrutinize every act, every statement emanating from London for signs of an insidious effort to destroy what remained of the rights of Englishmen. Many colonists knew about the tendency of all governments, even their own, to destroy liberty because they had already read Robert Trenchard and Thomas Gordon's *Cato's Letters*, published in book form in 1721. Trenchard and Gordon had forcefully outlined the dangers that liberty-loving people everywhere faced, no matter how virtuous their governments appeared to be on the surface. Nor did Americans have to peruse the dusty pages of commentators who had written decades earlier in order to give life to their suspicions. They had the word of prominent and well-placed Englishmen who assured them that the king's ministers were busily at work destroying the independence of the House of Commons—and that they were succeeding in their efforts.

One well-placed observer, in particular, had observed the ministry's machinations firsthand, and for a decade he had been warning both Englishmen and the colonists of the existence of a plot against liberty. Edmund Burke was more than a spectator at the Cockpit. It was he who had provided the colonies with some of the evidence indicating that the king's ministers had already destroyed parliamentary independence and now had set their sights on colonial liberties. Worries about a ministerial conspiracy began to surface almost as soon as George III ascended the throne in 1760 at the age of twenty-three. In 1762, the young and untested king appointed the unpopular John Stuart, 3rd Earl of Bute, as his chief minister. Bute, a Scotsman, had once served as George's tutor and he was one of the monarch's closest confidants at the beginning of his reign. In 1763 howls of protests concerning Bute's undue influence on George III, coupled with unfounded rumors about Bute's sexual relationship with George's mother, finally led the king to demand his mentor's resignation. But many in Parliament, including, ironically, George Grenville, were convinced that while Bute no longer held the formal reins of power, he nevertheless continued to have considerable malevolent influence behind the scenes.[17] He used that influence, of course, to subvert the English constitution and to make sure that anyone who disagreed with the king received no office and no favor. Only those who "slavishly" bowed to the monarch's every whim, Bute's detractors said, had a chance to succeed.[18]

Burke's suspicions did not abate when Bute stepped down from his office. He saw every chief minister but Rockingham and Pitt as dangerous, and he described in torrid prose the existence of a ministry-led "cabal of the closet and back-stairs" whose "designs" were destroying the balance between liberty and power.[19] The "court faction," as Burke referred to the men who dominated the government, was turning the very word "liberty" into an object of scorn.[20] Tories in the House, he wrote, gladly served the ministers, eager to count themselves as the "king's friends" in exchange for royal favor. Unfortunately, the conspirators were not only wicked, they were shrewd. They "proceeded gradually, but not slowly" in seeking the opportunity to "restore Royalty to its original splendour."[21] They never sought the very highest positions, fearing that doing so would draw attention to their plans. Instead, they gained posts "with art and judgement through all the secondary, but efficient, departments of office, and through the households of all the branches of the Royal Family."[22] Worst, they were succeeding, "driving hard to the ruin" of the country, "sapping the foundation of its liberty." Thus, the House of Commons was "totally corrupted," "indolent and submissive," abandoning the people's trust.[23] If Edmund Burke, an eyewitness to Parliament's behavior, was convinced of a ministerial conspiracy against liberty, how were the colonists to think otherwise?

Many in both England and America were accustomed to viewing government in conspiratorial terms. Thus they did not see Wedderburn's lurid depiction of secret plots and evil cabals as irrational or paranoid in and of itself. The question appeared to be, who was conspiring against whom? Was liberty in danger? Or was it authority or power that was most vulnerable? And for those who were most at risk, how were they to defend themselves against the designs of their enemies? The series of events that plagued Anglo-American relationships after 1763 led both Englishmen and colonists to view their fears of conspiracy from above or below with increasing seriousness. Those, like Franklin, who resisted such interpretations were increasingly either dismissed as incredibly naïve or simply ignored. Each event, each disagreement accelerated the sense of impending doom. None of those events alone was sufficient to lead Englishmen to the brink of war. It was the accumulation of controversies, each following close upon the heels of the other, that convinced leaders in England and the colonies that they had no choice but to defend themselves against those individuals whom they had once counted as their own countrymen.

Englishmen saw their efforts to gain control of an increasingly unwieldy empire as eminently reasonable. They worried whenever they heard that the mainland colonies were exhibiting signs of independence. They had also read the accounts of visitors to America who pointed out that the colonists were doing quite well financially and were surely able to contribute something to the nation's coffers without suffering unduly. As matters stood at the end of the Seven Years' War, the provinces were actually an economic burden, at a time when virtually everyone in England took it for granted that the colonies' sole purpose for existing was to contribute to the financial well-being of the mother country. There were estimates that it actually cost England 8,000 pounds to collect a mere 2,000 pounds in customs duties.[24] Something was definitely wrong with that picture. Now that England had emerged from the war victorious—if not prosperous—this seemed to be an opportune time to put imperial affairs in order.

From the perspective of most members of Parliament, there was simply no reason to ask whether or not England should gain control of its colonies. As they saw it, no government worthy of the name could sit idly by, watching its possessions spin out of control. Only a handful of men voted against the Sugar Act and Stamp Act, and none questioned Parliament's right to tax its own possessions. Grenville, himself, never deviated from his conviction that his legislation was completely legal. Nor did he think he was wrong to expect Americans to do just a little to relieve those in England who were already taxed to the hilt. He was disdainful of colonists who talked loudly about their "rights as Englishmen" but who remained strangely silent when anyone asked them to assume the duties that accompanied those rights. If Americans attacked Parliament's right to tax them, were they not implying that they were already independent?

The colonists, however, accustomed to governing and taxing themselves, were both frightened and appalled by what even Grenville conceded was an innovation. Americans from one end of the continent to the other were at least open to the suggestion that Grenville's legislation was a troubling indication that their rights were under attack and that their liberties were in danger. If Parliament could put its hands in colonial pockets whenever it needed money, then how could Americans defend their own property? Ironically, the very concessions the chief minister made to sweeten the pot made conspiracy-minded Americans more suspicious than ever. The taxes may not have been especially egregious, but that made them all the more insidious. If the colonists did not defend themselves in this instance, simply accepting the argument that they were not unduly burdened by the Stamp Act, they would allow Grenville to set a precedent. They would recognize England's claim that, in principle, Parliament had the right to tax them. If that happened, then England could return again and again, taking more and more money from subjects who were helpless to defend themselves. Soon they would be bereft of their property and unable to make a living. Massachusetts-born James Otis put the colonists' case as well as anybody:

> I can see no reason to doubt but that the imposition of taxes . . .
> in the colonies, is absolutely irreconcileable with the rights of the
> Colonists, as British subjects, and as men. I say men, for in a state of
> nature, no man can take my property from me, without my consent:
> If he does, he deprives me of my liberty, and makes me a slave.[25]

It went without saying that a government that enacted policies that led to the enslavement of its own people was a government that needed to be carefully watched.

The Stamp Act protests surprised most Englishmen. The petitions to king and Parliament and the boycott of British goods were unnerving enough. But the unchecked harassment of Stamp Distributors was frightening evidence that anarchy was spreading throughout the colonies. Andrew Oliver was the Distributor in Boston, and he was the first to find himself at the mercy of an angry crowd. The "mob" hanged him in effigy, razed his shops to the ground, and, according to Governor Bernard, threatened to kill him unless he renounced his position. Frightened and defenseless, Oliver complied. But assaults on property belonging to purported supporters of the Stamp Act (including, of course, Thomas Hutchinson) quickly spread. Soon Stamp Distributors were rushing to resign at the slightest hint of popular anger. By November 1, 1765, when the Act was to go into effect, the

legislation was a virtual dead-letter. Governors were impotent, forced
to watch as editors published their newspapers, courts in some colonies
opened for business, and merchants sailed in and out of the harbors
without buying a single stamp.

Not surprisingly, many English leaders viewed the repeal of the
Stamp Act with concern. King George III feared that the colonies had
degenerated into "licentiousness."[26] Repeal, worried some, gave every
appearance of "weakness and timidity in the Government and Parliament." It threatened to legitimize a "most dangerous doctrine, destructive to all Government," namely that no one, anywhere need obey any
law that offended anyone's "private judgment" that the legislation violated his rights.[27] Grenville was especially distraught. Franklin
observed with ill-disguised amusement that in the aftermath of repeal,
the former chief minister behaved "as if a little out of his Head on the
Article of America, which he brings into every Debate without Rhyme
or Reason." Even his friends were tired of his "harangues."[28] He talked
incessantly about the message that repeal had sent. England was helpless to enforce its own laws; colonial governors were disregarded at
best, threatened with physical harm at worst; the balance between liberty and power in America was tipping toward liberty. Anarchy would
be the result. Until he died, Grenville blamed the revocation of the
Stamp Act for all the difficulties that troubled Anglo-American relations after 1766. He was certain that by giving in to colonial protests
in this single instance, Parliament had signaled that England did not
have the fortitude to stand up to its out-of-control possessions. Consequently, Americans never again deferred to a government that could
not demand respect.

Neither the colonists nor Parliament had long to wait before each
was confirmed in its suspicions of the other. The Rockingham ministry dissolved almost as soon as the ink was dry on the Declaratory Act,
and it fell to the erratic Charles Townshend to deal with the government's budgetary red ink. When the colonists learned that the Chancellor of the Exchequer had persuaded Parliament to pass the
Townshend Acts, they were flabbergasted. They had convinced themselves that repeal was proof that public-spirited colonists could protect their liberties so long as they had the will and courage to do so.
Now it was apparent that England had not learned its lesson after all,
that it had not given up on its plan to destroy the rights of its own

people. This was, as many saw it, the third time in four years that Parliament had tried to tax them. It did not matter that this was an "external" tax, that it targeted luxury items that few could afford and that the wealthy could surely do without. It proved that government officials either did not understand the colonists' determination to protect their rights, or they did not care. Edmund Burke knew what he was talking about. The king's ministers were still exerting their influence in Parliament, England's lawmakers were corrupted, and the fate of liberty was in doubt. While some, like Franklin's friend and colleague Joseph Galloway, argued that the Sugar, Stamp, and Townshend acts, however wrong-headed, were discrete pieces of legislation designed to solve very real financial problems, many in America sensed that these acts were connected, that they were part of a deliberate effort to subvert colonial liberty.

But the British viewed the situation through the lens of their own conspiracy theory. Because he had scrupulously heeded Benjamin Franklin's contention that Americans would willingly pay external taxes, and because the colonists had always paid import duties without raising constitutional objections, Townshend was sure that his legislation would meet with no hostility. Most members of Parliament agreed, insisting that the colonists had absolutely nothing to complain about—unless, of course, they were determined to throw off their allegiance to England altogether. Protests could mean only one thing. No matter how reasoned their approach, no matter how they tried to craft legislation that the colonists would accept, they were met with stubborn rebuffs. It seemed as though Americans had no principles, as they continually changed the rules of the game to suit their own purposes. Either they were simply too selfish to contribute to the good of the Empire or, more ominously, malcontents were looking for any excuse to sow the seeds of discontent in their own domain. Thus, many began to suspect that those who feared that Americans were aiming at independence were right. Moreover, if Benjamin Franklin now—however mildly and carefully—condemned the Townshend Acts, then he might well be the least trustworthy, the most insidious colonist of all.

The response to the Townshend Acts escalated tensions and elevated suspicions. Under the circumstances, even minor incidents could have huge consequences. In 1768 a group of sailors and dockworkers in

Boston attacked customs inspectors bent upon enforcing the new legislation. Frightened, the inspectors fled to Castle William in the harbor, and they sent word home maintaining that they could not do their jobs in a city where anarchy ruled. Determined not to cave in to rioters once again, Lord Hillsborough ordered General Thomas Gage to send two regiments to Boston to restore order and protect the customs collectors from further harm.

While Englishmen worried about anarchy in Boston, Bostonians saw the royal troops in their midst as proof of what some had suspected all along. Those soldiers that the king had decided to keep in America at the end of the Seven Years' War were not there to enforce the Proclamation Line or to protect the colonists from Indian attack. They were really there looking for an opportunity to destroy American liberty. For two years, the troops remained in Boston. Their presence resulted in frustrations and resentments that were predictable and, no doubt, unavoidable. Fights broke out in the taverns and the streets. Soldiers moonlighted, taking jobs from ordinary townsmen. Men were harassed when they roamed the streets at night in defiance of the curfew. Soldiers and officers alike bought goods from local tradesmen and then refused to pay for their purchases. And the Red Coats were simply there, a very real and noticeable presence, stirring up anxiety in those who believed that deploying standing armies in a time of peace was a dangerous sign. Under the circumstances, words such as "tyranny" lost whatever abstract quality they might once have possessed. In Boston, they struck very close to home.

On March 5, 1770 hostilities broke out. Lieutenant Governor Hutchinson had feared just such an eventuality. He watched as tensions had escalated, at one point even begging Gage to withdraw most if not all of his troops. Incident after incident, each unrelated to the other, finally led to the confrontation that Hutchinson had tried to avert. When alarm bells sounded throughout the town on the night of March 5, Bostonians poured into the streets. They gradually made their way to King Street where a lone guard, Hugh White, stood sentinel, guarding the Customs House. Some carried clubs; others had picked up stones and large chunks of ice along the way. Finally they reached White, who had no chance to defend himself. Captain Thomas Preston and a small squad of soldiers rushed to protect the sentinel from the menacing crowd. Their muskets were at the ready even though Preston gave strict orders that no one was to fire. What happened next is anybody's guess. A shot rang out, others quickly followed, and when the dust had cleared, five men lay dead or dying, the victims of what silversmith Paul Revere labeled the "horrid massacre on King Street."

The reaction to the "massacre" was predictable. While many in the colonies were troubled by the mob action that had led to the debacle, others, especially in New England, saw the murder of innocents as unimpeachable proof that standing armies were dangerous to human life and to liberty itself. Englishmen were convinced that the "massacre" showed just how far unruly colonists were willing to go in their efforts to destroy all respect for law, order, and common decency. To the surprise and relief of most observers, however, in the three years following the "Boston Massacre" a deceptive calm pervaded the atmosphere. Everyone temporarily stepped back from the precipice.

Fortuitously, on the very day that the "massacre" took place Parliament was discussing the Townshend Acts. Much to the disgust of men of the ilk of George Grenville, the House repealed most of the Townshend Duties, retaining only the tax on tea. Hillsborough admitted that the tea tax had little practical value. It would not raise much money, and it would do nothing to regulate trade. But Parliament was determined to secure colonial recognition of the principles embedded in the Declaratory Act. Refusing to back down completely as it had done earlier, it retained the tea tax as a symbol of Parliament's sovereignty. Still, even the partial repeal of the Townshend Duties did a great deal to mollify most colonists. That Parliament never again introduced new taxes probably did as much as anything to ease tensions. It also helped that General Gage withdrew all of his troops from Boston. Was this, Members of Parliament asked, the behavior one might expect from a tyrannical government?

Boston's treatment of Captain Preston and those of his soldiers who were fingered as most responsible for the "massacre" also helped calm everyone down. Although there were those Bostonians, perhaps a majority, who demanded vengeance for the death of what they saw as innocent protesters, both Preston and his men received fair trials. John Adams surprised many and angered some when he agreed to act as the attorney for the accused. He did a masterful job. In the end, two soldiers received minor punishments; everyone else, including Preston, was fully exonerated, thus calling into question the assumptions of many Englishmen that the colonists had no respect for the law. With the troops gone, the trial over, and the bulk of the Townshend Duties off the books, most Americans seemed satisfied with even an imperfect victory. Although Franklin urged the colonists to continue their boycott of British goods until the tax on tea was lifted, enthusiasm for the effort waned. First one province, then another, began buying English imports. Some people even bought East India tea. Surely this was not what one would expect from people who were conspiring to declare independence. Indeed, when Thomas Hutchinson assumed the office of governor just a little over a year to the day after the "massacre," he hoped that the worst of the divisions that marred the relationship between the colonies and England were behind him.

Instead, the Tea Act and the Tea Party that followed in its wake ratcheted up hostilities once more. In retrospect, it seems clear that with the destruction of the East India tea, both England and the colonies finally reached the point of no return. Just as Benjamin Franklin's relationship with the mother country was permanently altered by his appearance at the Cockpit—an appearance that occurred within the context of government anger over the Tea Party—so, after December 1773, both England and America lost any chance they may have had to regain the trust that had once connected them to one another.

To a growing number of colonists, the Tea Act was proof that Parliament had not abandoned its desire to subjugate its mainland possessions. To most Englishmen, the Tea Party indicated that Americans would never accept Parliament's authority unless they were met with force. Parliament, they said, had backed down time and time again, only to be ignored and humiliated at every turn. Their efforts at compromise had been futile; the colonists had repeatedly taken advantage of their goodwill. Indeed, American demagogues had never been interested in anything but independence. One anonymous writer said it all, contending that it was "obvious, that they have no other view, than to throw off all subjection to this country. The idea has long been in embryo, and now emerges forth."[29] Virtually everyone agreed that a united front was essential if England was to have a chance to retain possession of its colonies. Thus it is no surprise that the Coercive Acts passed by an overwhelming majority. "The colonies," George III proclaimed somberly, "must either submit or triumph."[30] There was no middle ground.

Even as the king was issuing his ultimatum, delegates from the colonies met in Philadelphia to devise a strategy to persuade London to repeal the Coercive Acts. Members of what became known as the First Continental Congress relied on the same methods that they believed had worked in the past, calling for a complete cessation of trade between England and the colonies. They insisted that Massachusetts had no obligation to obey what they always called the "intolerable acts." But even though they were still talking—somewhat desperately—about a return to the status quo as it had existed before 1763, fewer were willing than they had been a decade earlier to look the other way when they perceived a threat to their liberties. They would no longer regard something like the Declaratory Act as an inconsequential gesture. They had been fooled by the power-hungry English government one too many times, and they would not be so easily duped again. If George III told them that they had to either "submit or triumph," they were increasingly less likely to submit.

The controversy surrounding the Hutchinson/Oliver letters brought Thomas Hutchinson's fears of a democratic conspiracy to the fore. By 1773, the governor thought he knew who was behind most if not all the catastrophic decisions that the colonists made. After he arrived in London, Hutchinson saw Franklin only once, in February 1775 when both men happened to be observers of a debate in the House of Commons.[31] But he saw his erstwhile friend's hand everywhere. He distrusted many other colonists, of course, especially those with whom he had dealt in Boston. He described Samuel Adams, for instance, as "a sort of Wilkes in New England" whose "pretended zeal for liberty" had intentionally prepared the way for independence.[32] But for Hutchinson, Benjamin Franklin had come to exist in a category all his own. When members of the Continental Congress fell to bickering among themselves, it was Franklin, the governor insisted, who persuaded them to bury their differences and work together.[33] Whenever Americans began to waver, it was Franklin again who promised his "deluded correspondents" that if they would just stand firm a bit longer, a huge "majority would be for them in the next Parliament."[34] Rumor had it that when the Continental Congress was preparing a dutiful petition to the king before disbanding for good, a letter from Franklin fortuitously arrived "which put an end to the Petition, and obtained a Vote

for Non-importation."[35] Hutchinson was sure that Franklin was inde-
fatigable, writing speeches for Lord Chatham, conveying congressional
petitions to Lord Dartmouth, and "stirring up a meeting of the Merchants in London" on the colonists' behalf.[36] When the governor himself tried to persuade Parliament to repeal at least some of the Coercive
Acts, he was met with blank stares. Once more his archenemy was to
blame. Franklin's letter to Congress "wishing or advising measures to
distress or ruin the Kingdom" had so angered Lord North—who
announced that the colonists were already "in actual Rebellion"—that
any compromise was unthinkable.[37]

As dangerous as Franklin was in England, Hutchinson feared that
if he ever went home he would excite the colonists "to still greater acts
of revolt."[38] Wedderburn agreed, commenting that someone should
stop Franklin from leaving England, hinting that prison was the
appropriate place for the once-respected American agent to spend the
rest of his days.[39] But even though Hutchinson and Wedderburn were
not alone in seeing Franklin as a "dangerous man," the leader of a "dangerous conspiracy" against the government, nothing was done to stop
him. To the contrary, Franklin sailed for home in the spring of 1775.[40]
He did not reach his destination until after the battles of Lexington
and Concord. But he knew, even before Minutemen and Red Coats
shed one another's blood on the fields of Massachusetts, that the end
of the Empire he loved was near.

Hutchinson surely exaggerated Benjamin Franklin's role in stirring the fires of rebellion. No one person can make a revolution in any
event. Until very late in the game, Franklin was not even close to being
the most radical colonial agitator. In fact Benjamin Franklin was the
one man standing at the Cockpit on January 29 who had generally
dismissed the conspiratorial language that emanated from both sides
of the Atlantic. No one, he believed—with the exception of those lone
turncoats, Thomas Hutchinson and Andrew Oliver—was conspiring
to destroy anyone. Indeed, if Franklin's own words are to be believed,
once he read the Hutchinson/Oliver letters, he became convinced that
if a conspiracy against liberty existed, it originated not in the corridors
of ministerial power but in America itself. To his mind, the letters
proved that colonial grievances "took their rise not from Government
here but were projected, proposed to Administration, solicited and
obtained by some of the most respectable among the Americans

themselves."⁴¹ Only after his humiliation at the Cockpit did Franklin come to the conclusion that colonial radicals were right. England was, indeed, bent on destroying colonial liberty. Hutchinson and Oliver may have been willing participants in the ministerial plot, but the king and his advisers were hardly unwitting pawns in a dangerous game.

Many historians have noted, and tried to explain, Franklin's skeptical view of conspiracy theories. Why, they ask, did he not see what Englishmen and Americans both observed without even trying? Some insist that the American agent was simply a confirmed moderate who thought most men were as reasonable as he was. He was, then, someone who always believed compromise among men of goodwill was possible. This explanation may have some validity. Still, as his quarrel with Thomas Penn surely indicates, Franklin was not always cool and rational. He was quite capable of seeing evidence of ill will in those he designated as his enemies, and he had no qualms about engaging those enemies in a battle to the finish. Others argue that Franklin—like Burke—disliked discussions about abstract concepts such as "rights" and "liberty." That being the case, the fevered language of those whose zeal to protect colonial liberties allowed their paranoia to get the better of them held no appeal for him. But Franklin was no stranger to abstract discussions about the meaning and structure of the British Empire. Indeed, one can fairly argue that it was his concept of the Empire, coupled with his own experiences in England and the colonies, that led him—until very late—to brush aside the conspiratorial diatribes that emanated from his friends on both sides of the Atlantic. Franklin did not believe that Americans wanted independence or that the king's ministers wanted to enslave the colonies. Throughout the sixties and well into the seventies he deplored what he saw as "Imprudencies on both Sides." But "imprudencies" were hardly plots. His greatest fear was that "Step by Step," men who had the very best intentions would behave in ways that would "bring on the most mischievous Consequences."⁴² To a great extent, this was because he knew England better than most Americans did and he understood the colonies in ways that escaped most Englishmen.

Franklin was, in the language of the day, a thoroughgoing "Empire man." Although he always celebrated the optimism and vitality of his native land, this son of an emigrant was remarkably proud of his own English roots. In the summer of 1758, when he and his son William were in London, the two men embarked upon a sentimental trip through the countryside. They journeyed to their ancestral home in Willingborough in Northhamptonshire, where they were regaled with stories about those of their relatives who had not rejected old England in favor of the new. From Willingborough they moved on to Ecton, the birthplace of Josiah Franklin. There they encountered the rector's wife, who was kind enough to accompany them to the local cemetery where William dutifully copied inscriptions from the family gravestones and both men were entertained by still more tales of their ancestors. Their excursion gave father and son alike a palpable sense of their connection to the mother country, a link with the past that neither man could imagine that they would one day be asked to relinquish.

When Franklin sailed to England for the third—and as it turned out the last—time in 1764, the Pennsylvania Assembly had instructed him to protect his colony not only against the ploys of the Pennsylvania Proprietors but also from the designs of the king's ministers and, if need be, Parliament as well. He gladly promised to do so. But while he always defended the colonies' interests, it took him a very long time to concede that colonial needs and English imperatives were not only different but diametrically opposed. He found it impossible to agree with those who were sure that the Crown's ministers, in league with their spineless supporters in Parliament, were out to destroy American liberty. He was too much of a loyal servant of the king to believe that this was the case. Franklin knew England and Englishmen, and as a consequence he understood government policy even when he did not agree with it.

Benjamin Franklin was no provincial. As a young man, he had lived in England for eighteen pleasurable months when he was still trying to figure out what to do with his life. He returned in 1757, remaining there five years, long after it had become apparent that his quarrel with the Pennsylvania Proprietors would come to no satisfactory end. This time he had arrived, not as a slightly bewildered boy on the make, but as a man whose intellectual credentials had dazzled men of letters throughout western Europe. He had already conducted his famous kite experiment, and he was becoming known everywhere as "the man who tamed the lightning." His short book—only eighty-six pages—describing his findings, *Experiments and Observations on Electricity, Made at Philadelphia in America*, had gone through five English editions and was also published in France, Italy, and Germany. He had been admitted to membership in London's prestigious Royal Society, an honor few Englishmen and even fewer colonials ever attained. Once in England he was wined and dined, feted and celebrated, even receiving honorary degrees from the University at St. Andrews and Oxford University. It is no wonder that he left for home in 1762 with deep reluctance. He may have missed his wife and daughter, but he promised his friend, London printer William Strahan, that he would soon return to London, and this time he would "settle here for ever."[43]

Nor did absence from England make his heart grow any less fond. Philadelphia's cultural offerings may have been vibrant and sophisticated by colonial standards, but they did not begin to compare with London's. "Of all the enviable Things England has," he wrote Mary Stevenson, his London landlady's daughter, "I envy it most its People. Why should that petty Island, which compar'd to America is but a stepping Stone in a Brook . . . why, I say, should that little Island, enjoy in every Neighbourhood more sensible, virtuous, and elegant Minds than we can collect in ranging 100 Leagues of our vast Forests?" True enough the colonies would one day boast achievements that would be the envy of the world. But for the present, America was an unimpressive backwater.[44] Thus Franklin was not unhappy when, after less than two years in Philadelphia, he set sail for England once more. There he remained for ten, mostly happy years, making increasingly perfunctory promises to return to Philadelphia but never quite managing to pack up his belongings and head for home.

Franklin's love for England was based on more than the friends he made, the honors he received, and the stimulating conversations he enjoyed so long as he remained there. He had devoted much of his adult life to the service of king and country. He did so not simply because he was ambitious, but because he sincerely believed that Englishmen on both sides of the water would benefit from seeing themselves "not as belonging to different Communities with different Interests, but to one Community with one Interest." This "would contribute to strengthen the whole, and greatly lessen the danger of future separations."[45] True enough, he predicted, America—with a population that increased exponentially every year, and a huge expanse of land ripe for exploitation by eager and capable colonists—would eventually surpass England in importance, laying the "Foundations of the future Grandeur and Stability of the British Empire." Nevertheless, he contended that only if England and America acted in concert would they be able to build a society that would "awe the World."[46] It was for that reason that he was one of a handful of Americans who supported Governor Bernard's suggestion that England grant representation in Parliament to the colonies.

Significantly, Franklin invariably looked to the king whenever he discussed the ties that bound the Empire together. He assumed that it was to the king, not Parliament, that Americans owed their loyalty. The monarch, after all, was the source of authority for all of the colonies. It was the king who accepted or rejected provincial law. Until the middle of the seventeenth century, Parliament had virtually ignored America; even after that time, although it had enacted occasional laws regulating provincial trade, it left most colonial policy to the Crown. And it was the king—at least until 1764—who asked the individual legislatures for monetary support for the wars the colonies fought in his name.

Franklin was a royalist throughout the 1760s. In 1761, he and his son cut short their vacation to rush to London in time to attend George III's coronation. His praise for England's monarch—the first Hanoverian king to have been born in England, the first fluent in the English language—was fulsome. "Never," he said, had England had a "better prince," and he fearlessly predicted that the king's reign would be both "happy and glorious."[47] As late as 1770 Franklin assured the colonists that the monarch had "the best Disposition towards us, and has a Family-Interest in our Prosperity." Indeed, the path to the preservation of colonial liberties lay in America's "steady Loyalty" to the king.[48] It was not really until George III rejected the Continental Congress's petition against the Coercive Acts that Franklin reluctantly conceded in public that he could not blame either Parliament or the king's advisers alone for the various efforts to tax the colonies. Some of the onus lay on the king's own shoulders. Still, it took an extraordinarily long time for Franklin to reach that point. Even as colonial leaders shuddered and King George's men fumed, until 1774 Benjamin Franklin refused to countenance the fears on either side.

That Franklin was proud of his English heritage, and that he truly admired George III, the best of all monarchs, at least in part explains his reluctance to give much credence to the conspiratorial rhetoric that came almost as second nature to most of his countrymen. His experiences in England gave him even more reason to doubt that the colonies were under siege. Unlike most Americans, even those wealthy enough to visit London on occasion, Franklin was completely at home in England. He moved in august circles. He knew personally many of the men whom political leaders back home decried as would-be tyrants, and while he grew to despise a few, he was aware that some were friends of America and most others had no desire to destroy colonial liberty. They may have been misguided and stubborn, and perhaps some of them were not very bright, but they were not evil.

Thus, even when he was frustrated by government policy, Franklin always found reason to be hopeful. Certain that the English people, if not the English government, sympathized with the colonies, he insisted that there was "much good will towards America in the generality" of England.[49] "The popular Inclination here," he would say confidently, "is, to wish us well, and that we may preserve our Liberties." He could not believe that the country's leaders would defy the "Sense of the Nation" forever.[50]

Franklin was always sure that the Members of Parliament were gaining a "general Sense of our growing Importance, a Disapprobation of the harsh Measures with which we have been treated, and a Wish that some Means may be found of perfect Reconciliation." Year after year he claimed to see unmistakable signs that the "Friends of Liberty" were about to gain control of the government.[51] In 1771, for instance, he painted a rosy picture of the Empire's future for Massachusetts Speaker Thomas Cushing. While he conceded that the Bay Colony had suffered at Parliament's hands in recent years, he predicted that this was about to change. Those who were determined to "abuse" the colonies were in the minority, he insisted; America's supporters were coming into their own. It would take a while before England would lift the tea tax; it would take even longer for Parliament to renounce its claim to the right to tax its mainland possessions. Even so, he was sure that the government would make no further attempt actually to do what it steadily claimed it had a right to do. Moreover, time was on the colonies' side. If Americans would refrain from offering any "fresh occasion" to incur England's wrath, their "growing importance" would eventually "compel an acknowledgement" of their rights, and "establish and secure them to our posterity."[52]

Franklin knew firsthand what Americans did not always appreciate. English politics was extremely volatile. That very volatility, however difficult to control in the short run, promised to work in the colonists' favor in the end. Nothing lasted. What looked like a disaster one day could easily be forgotten the next. A suspect officeholder, a Bute or a Grenville or a Hillsborough, could do considerable damage. But cooler heads inevitably prevailed. The friends of the colonies always had a chance to regain the upper hand. True enough, the "perpetual permutations" and the incessant "confusion among our Great Men" was excruciatingly frustrating.[53] But the constant "Changes of Men and Minds" often helped men like Franklin who were adept at using factional infighting for their own ends. In the spring of 1770, he described the situation to a friend. "The Ministry," he said, "are not all of a Mind, nor determin'd what are the next Steps proper to be taken with us." Some demanded severity; others were for "lenient Measures." No one could predict the outcome. So long as that was true, talk of a unified ministerial conspiracy against liberty was idle chatter and nothing more.[54]

Franklin saw the resignation of Lord Hillsborough in 1772 as proof that he was right to be hopeful. Hillsborough was replaced by William Legge, Lord Dartmouth, Lord North's half-brother. In 1765 Franklin had described Dartmouth as a "young Man of excellent Understanding and the most amiable Dispositions."[55] He had no reason to alter his opinion once Dartmouth assumed office. He was delighted when the secretary greeted him "very obligingly" and, unlike his predecessor, did not object to his "irregular" appointment by the Massachusetts Assembly. Thus Franklin looked forward to "being able to obtain more in favour of our Colonies upon occasion" than he had been able to do in quite some time.[56] Only reluctantly did he come to the conclusion that Dartmouth's words were more promising than his deeds. "He is truly a good Man," Franklin wrote his son, "and wishes sincerely a good Understanding with the Colonies, but does not seem to have Strength equal to his Wishes."[57] Even so, while weakness was disappointing, it did not reveal wicked intent.

Nor did Franklin believe that a plot to secure independence existed on the other side of the Atlantic. Although he lived in England for a decade, Franklin kept in touch with a wide variety of people at home. As an agent, of course, he was in constant contact with colonial leaders. He also received regular updates from his son and from Joseph Galloway. By 1770 he heard more and more often from Massachusetts activists, getting a perspective that was more critical of the English government than any he had received earlier on. But no matter how often he heard Englishmen speak darkly of the colonial lust for independence, Franklin knew they were wrong. He freely admitted that a few hotheads at home were a little rash, that some excused or even promoted violence on occasion. But he knew that the most radical colonists did not want to destroy the bonds that tied them to the Empire. To the contrary, Americans were unmatched in their love of England and even more in their reverence for the king. Where Englishmen in England were a little jaded, as likely to mock their Hanoverian rulers as they were to praise them, the colonists, like Franklin himself, clung passionately to the ties that bound them to the monarchy. Ordinary Americans filled their houses with objects bearing the likeness of the king—glasses, mugs, portraits, wax effigies. All of these items contributed to what one historian has called the "royalization of private life" in the colonies.[58] It was unthinkable to imagine that people whose affection for England knew no bounds were conspiring to destroy the Empire.

Moreover, even if some colonists did harbor a secret desire for independence—a possibility that Franklin firmly rejected—no one who understood America could believe that would-be rebels could achieve their ends. Englishmen painted "the colonies" with a broad brush, but Franklin knew how divided and fractured his countrymen really were. It was the colonial assemblies after all, each determined to preserve its autonomy, that had rejected his Albany Plan. Even those colonies that eagerly supported the king's army during the French and Indian War had eyed one another with suspicion, refusing to pay more for defense than anyone else, always trying to get the best deal for themselves often at one another's expense. In the period between 1770 and 1773, all Franklin's arts of persuasion were not enough to keep Americans from bickering over matters large and small. They quarreled over boundary lines. They fought with one another over access to the very western lands that the Franklins and their allies were eyeing with such avidity. They were incapable of enforcing the nonimportation agreement once Parliament had repealed most of the Townshend Duties. It was laughable to think that the colonists were capable of fomenting a conspiracy resulting in independence.

After his experience at the Cockpit, however, Franklin's views began to change. He continued to disparage those who talked of a colonial plot to attain independence. But he much more often agreed that England was out to destroy colonial liberty. Two weeks after his humiliation he was still smarting, barely able to discuss an event that filled him with "resentment" and left him "very angry." Indeed he had not been this furious since his fight so long ago with the Penns. In both cases, he felt personally humiliated. And in both cases, his famous penchant for compromise simply evaporated. He admitted that for once he was "at a loss to know how peace and union is to be maintained or restored between the different parts of the empire." If the colonists were no longer allowed even to complain or to submit petitions asking for reform, then independence might be the only remaining option.[59] As Franklin saw it, the ministers' cavalier rejection of the golden opportunity he had offered them to turn Hutchinson and Oliver into "Scape-Goats" was evidence enough that the king's men were not acting in good faith. "They might have thanked me," he said tersely. Instead they chose to "abuse me."[60]

After the Cockpit, Franklin's mood darkened and his susceptibility to conspiratorial notions was increasingly apparent. Less than a month after his ordeal, he wrote to Thomas Cushing, indicating that he was convinced that the entire charade was "preconcerted." How else, he demanded, could any one explain the huge number of "courtiers" who were present that day, "invited as to an entertainment?" For what other reason had the Privy Councilors sat quietly, allowing Wedderburn to attack him—the mere messenger—instead of addressing the merits of the Massachusetts petition? He also believed that William Whately was suing him in chancery court at "the instance of the ministry." Left to his own devices, Whately would never have behaved so dishonorably. At the very least, North and his minions were doing all they could to harass him and they might, he hinted, even be seeking to arrest and imprison him.[61]

More and more, after January 1774, Franklin began making the arguments that other colonial leaders had been advancing since the mid-sixties. In less contentious times, for instance, he had defended England against provincial depictions of a British government riddled with corruption, assuring English botanist Peter Collinson, "you have a great deal of Virtue still subsisting among you."[62] And he had remarked to Joseph Galloway that England was "not so near a dissolution, as some seem to apprehend."[63] After the Cockpit, however, Franklin decried English corruption from the rooftops. Aspiring Members of Parliament, he maintained, regularly bought or bribed their way into seats of power, and then were reduced to "selling their Votes to the Minister for the time being, to reimburse themselves."[64] The king's ministers, moreover, were "dissipate in Corruption," even lying to their own countrymen in an effort to foment a war with the colonies that was not in the nation's best interest.[65] Where once he had dreamed of a strong and united Empire that served Englishmen everywhere, he now thought separation was essential if America was to remain untouched by English venality. "When I consider the extream Corruption prevalent among all Orders of Men in this old rotten State," he said, "and the glorious publick Virtue so predominant in our rising Country, I cannot but apprehend more Mischief than Benefit from a closer Union." If the colonies did not dissolve their connection to England, they would be overrun by "Injustice and Rapacity" as well as "Prodigality and Profusion." Otherwise, he darkly predicted, English habits would inevitably "corrupt and poison us also."[66] Objectively speaking, England was no more venal in 1775 than it had been ten years earlier. England had not changed, at least not drastically. Benjamin Franklin had.

In the months following the Cockpit, Franklin came as close as he ever had to believing that a conspiracy against liberty had existed for some time. The king's ministers, he said, had engaged in a "Series of iniquitous and irritating Measures," deliberately provoking "a loyal People almost to Desperation." As a result, war was likely, not because the colonists wanted it, but because of "ministerial Pique and Obstinacy."[67] He continued to hold out a glimmer of hope for reconciliation. He desperately wanted to believe that only a relatively few—unfortunately well-placed—men were preparing to place the yoke of tyranny on all Americans. But he had reluctantly come to agree with his radical counterparts that there were more in London than he had been willing to admit who were determined to "enslave" the colonies.[68] By the time he finally left London in the spring of 1775, he was morally certain that Lord North's administration had no desire for reconciliation, even under the most favorable terms. He thought "that they rather wish'd to provoke the N[ew] E[ngland] People into an open Rebellion, which might justify a military Execution, and thereby gratify a grounded Malice" against Whigs, dissenters, and lovers of liberty everywhere.[69]

True, Franklin continued to go through the motions so long as he remained in London. When various Englishmen approached him through circuitous channels, hoping to find some means of arriving at reconciliation, he played along. What, after all, did he have to lose? He was now a private man; he no longer represented any colony and spoke for no one but himself. The men who sought him out were equally powerless. Quakers David Barclay and John Fothergill, longtime friends of Franklin, were desperate to avoid war at any cost. Thomas Villiers, Baron Hyde was a member of the Privy Council, and he, too, was looking for a way to effect a compromise before it was too late. Admiral Richard, Lord Howe also participated in negotiations with Franklin. And then of course there was William Pitt, now Lord Chatham, who, when his health permitted it, had always been one of the colonies' most spirited defenders. But none of these people, not even Chatham, would listen to what Franklin saw as nonnegotiable demands. They refused to entertain any suggestion that parliamentary power was limited or that the colonial assemblies were autonomous entities, equal in their own spheres to Parliament itself. In fact, discussions of imperial affairs with men who counted themselves as sympathetic to the colonies made him realize, as never before, that it was impossible to bridge the gap dividing England and America. And so he sailed for home.

CHAPTER 5

....

Civil War

H is experience at the Cockpit put Benjamin Franklin on the trajectory toward embracing independence. But it did more than that. It signaled the beginning of the end not only of his proud connection to the Empire but also of his deep, emotional relationship to his own son. Just four days after his humiliation Benjamin wrote to William. The letter was terse and to the point. He scribbled a "Line" to report that he had just been relieved of his position at the post office. Consequently, he continued, it was obvious that William had lost any chance he may have had to improve his own prospects. Nor was his governorship of New Jersey, where his salary was a mere pittance and always had been, worth hanging on to. "I wish you were well settled in your Farm," Franklin concluded. "Tis an honester and a more honourable because a more independent Employment."[1]

While Franklin signed his note "Your affectionate Father," his message was not particularly kind. In a few brief sentences he implied that William's prospects were totally dependent on his connections with his father and that he could not hope for any other preferment without Benjamin's help. He also reminded his son that despite his valiant efforts over the years to secure a raise or a more lucrative post for himself, he had always failed. And Benjamin clearly expected William to share his own resentment of his ordeal and to resign his governorship in protest. Two weeks later, Benjamin sent a second letter to New Jersey, letting William off the hook, saving him—temporarily—from having to choose between loyalty to his father and retaining his position as royal governor. Rumor had it that William was about to be fired. Thus, Benjamin thought his son should sit tight. Hold on to your job, he advised, "tho," he could not resist adding, "in truth I think it scarce worth your keeping," and do not "save them the shame of depriving you whom they ought to promote."[2] Three months later, Benjamin changed his mind once again, warning William that he would live to regret it if he did not retire. "I think," he said pointedly, "Independence more honourable than any Service."[3] William Franklin never so much as acknowledged Benjamin's mixed messages. Instead he forged steadily ahead, clinging to a job that had long since helped shape his very identity. He had no intention of stepping down; he was not fired. And Benjamin wisely let the matter drop, never broaching the subject again.

Thus began the slow, painful, and seemingly inexorable process that would end in the destruction of the Empire that father and son loved, and of a personal relationship that both men had once valued above all others. For Benjamin and William Franklin, the American Revolution became not just a war for independence, but a civil war. Nor was their situation unique. Their experience, while particularly dramatic, was replicated in homes throughout America as men and women were forced to choose between their loyalty to England and their fealty to their own colony, and between their own views and the sentiments of other members of their family. While most Americans opted for independence, others—perhaps as many as 20 percent— were convinced that a separation from England was unnecessary, dangerous, and wrong.

When Americans hear references to "the Civil War," the nineteenth-century struggle between the forces of the Confederacy and the Union almost automatically springs to mind. Those with a romantic bent think sadly of a time when brother fought brother and father fought son on the blood-soaked fields of Gettysburg or Shiloh. Nevertheless, while there is an element of truth in this popular portrayal of the Civil War, relatively few families were actually divided by that conflict. True, families that inhabited the border states were sometimes torn asunder in the wake of the shots fired at Fort Sumter. There were also instances when fathers, brothers, and sons lived in different parts of the country. In the decades after the Revolution, many New Englanders, for instance, abandoned the rocky soil of

Massachusetts or New Hampshire in favor of the fertile cotton fields of Mississippi or Texas. Once there, they found themselves separated ideologically and economically from loved ones who did not follow them to the South. Still, it is fair to say that, as a whole, Americans embraced the beliefs of the men and women with whom they lived and worked every day. New Englanders were highly unlikely to don a uniform of Confederate Gray; white inhabitants of the deep South did not rush to join the Union Army. Brothers were much more apt to fight side-by-side than they were to face one another across the trenches.

In fact, the American Revolution can more accurately be described as a "civil war" than its nineteenth-century counterpart. The war for independence was actually a civil war in two ways. First, as many people at the time noted, when English colonists fought the Red Coats, they were engaging in a battle with their own countrymen. Although residents of England may have seen Americans as something of a different—and inferior—species, Americans themselves, a majority of them anyway, saw themselves as every bit as "English" as the king's subjects across the Atlantic. The war, claimed Massachusetts writer and staunch Patriot Judith Sargent Murray, was unnatural. It involved men and women who came from the "same stock"; those soldiers who entered the battle were, whether they recognized it or not, preparing to commit "fratricide."[4]

The American Revolution was a civil war in a narrower and much more painful sense as well. No colony avoided hostilities between Loyalists and Patriots. In every region, the conflict forced towns, churches, and schools to face these schisms. Although it was less likely, individual families, such as the Franklins, were rent by differences so strong that their members found themselves on opposite sides. Prominent Gloucester merchant Epes Sargent, for instance, remained loyal to the king, while his son and all his siblings supported the Patriot cause. At the beginning of the war, he and his wife fled the town of their birth, fearing retribution from the local Committee of Safety. Robert Beverley of Virginia was not a Loyalist, but neither was he a Patriot, much to the disgust of his father-in-law, planter Landon Carter. While Beverley was fortunate enough to escape punishment for his neutrality, his criticism of colonial resistance drew the wrath of members of his own family and most of his neighbors.

No matter what side people chose, they all valued their connection to England and they all wanted what was best for the colonies. Until the end, they hoped against hope that somehow they could find a way to retain both their loyalty and their liberties. And yet at some point they had to choose. Some went one way, some went another. Men and women, elite Americans and ordinary colonists, free people and slaves wound up on both sides of the divide. There were as many reasons for opting for one position over the other as there were people who took those positions. Some were moved by self-interest, others by hope or fear, some by relatives or friends, others by religious or philosophical beliefs. The Franklins' story was uniquely its own, of course. Nevertheless, it serves as a dramatic, even a tragic, reminder that the most radical Americans did not take independence lightly, and the most dedicated loyalists continued to love the colonies whose cause they opposed. They all struggled as they decided where their ultimate loyalties lay. No one viewed support for independence or loyalty to the Crown as a given.

In the beginning, Benjamin and William Franklin were as close—personally and ideologically—as a father and son could hope to be. They had so much in common: a love of England and a veneration of their English ancestors; loyalty to king and Empire and disapproval of parliamentary taxation; pride in their royal sinecures and a respect for the rights of colonial assemblies; a desire to exploit the resources of America's vast hinterland; an aversion to political extremes; and—unfortunately for their relationship—an unwillingness to sit on the sidelines once a quarrel was joined.

Although he may never have recognized it, much less admitted it, Benjamin Franklin was largely responsible for his son's continued loyalty to the king. Over the years William learned a great deal from his father, and he learned it all very well. While Benjamin declared that his early experiences in Boston led him to distrust authority, he gave his son every reason to believe that authority was wise and beneficent. Benjamin also taught William that England and America shared a common heritage and common interests, and thus that it was possible to serve colony and Empire simultaneously. "No Office or Honour in the Power of the Crown to bestow," Governor Franklin told the members of the New Jersey Assembly, "will ever influence me to forget or neglect the Duty I owe my Country, nor the most furious Rage of the most intemperate Zealots induce me to swerve from the Duty I owe his Majesty."[5] These were words that Benjamin Franklin could easily have uttered, at least until his appearance at the Cockpit.

Benjamin described himself as an "indulgent" father, and in most ways he was.[6] He raised William in relative affluence, and he was eager to give his son the advantages he himself had not enjoyed. William had his own pony; he had the benefit of a classical education; he moved in rarified circles in Philadelphia society. Thanks to Benjamin, despite his illegitimate birth and his own father's humble beginnings, William was accepted early on by the sons and daughters of the city's elite. Although he had little to complain about, as a youth he tried to run away from home, planning to board a privateer resting in the harbor. Benjamin quickly put a halt to his son's fancies, but he resolutely shunned the role of a tyrant, thus giving William no reason to rebel against his authority. Instead, he carefully steered the boy's penchant for adventure into more appropriate and socially rewarding channels. During the 1740s, the War of Austrian Succession (which the colonists called King George's War) was being waged in America as well as in Europe. What better way existed for William to serve the common good and get the itch for excitement out of his system than to join the military? With his father's help, William obtained an appointment as an ensign in the king's army. He loved military life, reluctantly leaving the army at war's end only after it became apparent that he had no realistic "Prospect of Advancement" in an institution that catered to men with money or connections or both.[7] Significantly, William's first effort to support himself came as a defender of king and Empire—and he did so with his father's blessing.

Once William returned from the front, the two men were inseparable. They joined the same clubs and supported the same charities. William was his father's only confidant when Benjamin conducted his famous kite experiment. As Benjamin continued to take charge of his son's career, he sent William one consistent message: loyalty to king and support of the Empire was a good thing. In 1750, he set William to work studying law under the direction of Philadelphia attorney Joseph Galloway, also registering him in London's Middle Temple where he would go one day to put the finishing touches on his professional education. Father and son traveled to the Albany Conference, where William observed firsthand the difficulties even the most adept political operatives faced whenever they tried to get the insular colonies to act in unison. During the French and Indian War, the two men worked together to secure supplies for General Edward Braddock's expedition to western Pennsylvania.

Of course Benjamin took his son with him to London in 1757, where, in the words of printer William Strahan, Benjamin was at once William's "friend, his brother, his intimate and easy companion."[8] The two men were a team, collaborating on an antiproprietary tract and frequenting the corridors of power where they sought sympathy for their goals. William shared his father's hatred of the Penns, and he wholeheartedly endorsed the plan to turn Pennsylvania into a royal colony. Further, in 1762 William used Benjamin's influence to obtain a

Mather Brown, *William Franklin*, 1790. Courtesy of the Frick Art Reference Library, used with permission from Ann C. Boswell.

colonial governorship. Not many Americans, especially ones who were so young and untried, could even hope to be a royal governor. Granted, New Jersey was not an especially important colony, but it was a beginning. Who knew, if he played his cards right, what preferments might come his way in the future?

After 1764, the Franklins lived on opposite sides of the Atlantic, but they derived pleasure and benefited from their close relationship for more than a decade. Benjamin returned to London determined to secure Crown control of Pennsylvania. William remained in New Jersey, working assiduously to maintain good relationships with both assembly and king, struggling to balance local concerns and imperial imperatives even as tempers began to fray. Theirs was a true partnership as each helped the other in myriad ways. William was the surrogate head of the Franklin household, regularly looking in on his stepmother and his sister. He visited Philadelphia often, serving as his father's eyes and ears, letting Benjamin know just which way the political winds at home were blowing. He also took care of routine business, a task that grew more demanding as Deborah's health failed and her ability to tend to the most routine matters declined. And he was there—when Benjamin was not—on a frigid December day in 1774 to watch as his "poor old Mother's" coffin was lowered into Philadelphia's icy ground.⁹

Benjamin was as useful to William as William was to Benjamin. He reminded his son to get his reports to the Board of Trade on time, often suggesting ways to make them more palatable to English authorities. He worked long and hard, if unsuccessfully, to persuade the ministry to approve the various projects William proposed to establish a colony west of the Proclamation Line. He supported his son's efforts to secure an independent salary. He offered his sage advice, suggesting tactics that William might use in his dealings with the New Jersey Assembly and with London officials. More than once William routed his letters to Lord Hillsborough through his father, asking him to look them over and make any alterations that he thought necessary before sending them on their way. Benjamin was helpful in more personal ways as well. While he was in London, William had imitated his father's example, siring an illegitimate son, William Temple Franklin. William did not acknowledge Temple as his child; thus, Benjamin kept a close eye on his grandson, assuming responsibility for his education.

The Franklins' partnership was not based solely on the mutual need to take care of business. The two men were in fundamental agreement on most matters. Both, for instance, were happy to serve the king, and eagerly sought better preferments than the ones they already enjoyed. William always hoped to use New Jersey as a springboard for more lucrative positions, a prospect his father unambiguously supported. Benjamin also looked out for himself. He did not spend his entire time in London representing the interests of the colonies who took him on as agent. Throughout the 1760s, even as he haunted the offices of London officials lobbying for Crown rule in Pennsylvania or trying to persuade one ministry after another to support his son's various speculative schemes, the elder Franklin was also angling for royal favor for himself. On more than one occasion, he was confident that he would succeed. In 1768, there was talk that he would secure a position under Lord Hillsborough, who had just ascended to the American Department. Later that year, Secretary to the Treasury Grey Cooper suggested that he might get a position in the Duke of Grafton's government. When Benjamin actually met briefly with Lord North, then Chancellor of the Exchequer, to discuss the matter, North assured him that he would do what he could to "find some way of making it worth your while" to remain in England.[10] Although Franklin tried to pretend that he was too old to harbor any personal ambition, he also admitted that he would turn down no offer that came his way. And he was clearly disappointed when nothing actually materialized. His appearance at the Cockpit put an end to his aspirations once and for all. Some of the men who had once promised to promote his interests were the very ones who laughed and jeered at Wedderburn's pointed barbs.

Throughout the 1760s both Franklins were certain that no conflict existed between loyalty to the king and a defense of colonial liberties. Nor did they imagine that their own occasional disagreements presaged a time when their close relationship would end. During the Stamp Act crisis, for instance, father and son agreed on the essentials. Both thought the Grenville administration should never have tried to tax the colonies. They also believed that taxation without representation was unconstitutional, even as they sought to avoid discussion of the principles involved. The Franklins wanted above all else to remain in the good graces of George III and his advisers. William, of course, was a royal governor who had sworn an oath of loyalty to the king. He was also a lawyer who could never countenance disobedience to the law, however distasteful that law might be. To complicate matters, he was as invested in the plan for altering Pennsylvania's government as his father was. Both men believed that if New Jersey did not directly oppose the Stamp Act, they could use the colony as a shining example of the virtues of royal government. Thus father and son, future loyalist and future patriot, lent their qualified support to the Crown throughout the early stages of the Stamp Act crisis.

They were also firm in their distaste for violent protest. When Benjamin worried about the "Rashness" of the petitions against the Stamp Act, and condemned the "Madness of the Populace" whose "rebellious Tendency" could "only bring themselves and Country into Trouble," William agreed.[11] Benjamin knew, of course, that the Proprietors were doing all they could to discredit him but he did not have to face his accusers in person. William did. He traveled so often to Philadelphia to defend his father that the Penns accused him of meddling in Pennsylvania affairs. He was, they said, working to repress liberty both in his native colony and his adopted one. William worried that his father's house would be pulled down by an angry mob and that his own governor's mansion would suffer a similar fate. Like his father, he walked a tightrope. He tried—and ultimately failed—to secure New Jersey's compliance with the Stamp Act. But he also avoided the "Officiousness" that other governors exhibited. He firmly believed that it would be a "Piece of Quixotism" to go on record in support of the Stamp Act. Doing so would "answer no good Purpose whatever." Whatever his personal views, he had no desire to become "obnoxious" to the people of New Jersey.[12] Thus father and son were overjoyed when Parliament repealed the Stamp Act. True to form, William made sure that everyone knew about Benjamin's part in securing that repeal.

Throughout the 1760s, father and son were usually on the same page. Neither man was unduly concerned by the Townshend Acts at first. Benjamin came to understand the colonial position. Because he knew firsthand what American leaders had always said about taxation without representation, so did William. While Benjamin was often able to ignore the controversy altogether, William had to deal with its consequences virtually every day. Indeed, he came as close as he ever

David Martin, *Benjamin Franklin*, 1767. Courtesy of the Pennsylvania Academy of the Fine Arts, Philadelphia. Gift of Maria McKean Allen and Phebe Warren Downes through the bequest of their mother, Elizabeth Wharton McKean.

would to losing his job altogether as an indirect result of the colonial reaction to the Townshend Duties. In early 1768, his assembly was in session when it received the letter from the Massachusetts House suggesting a united stance against the new legislation. New Jersey's lawmakers agreed. Lord Hillsborough was furious. Although William apologized profusely for his legislators' indiscretion, insisting that no one meant either king or Parliament any disrespect, Hillsborough was not mollified. Instead, he sent a stinging letter to Franklin, berating him for every breach of duty that he could dredge up. He accused both governor and assembly of assaulting parliamentary supremacy, implying that the colony's positive response to the Massachusetts missive was tantamount to rebellion.

Convinced that he would soon be fired, William sent a long, rambling letter to Hillsborough, defending himself and—significantly—his colony. Unusually candid, he blamed England, not New Jersey, for the current impasse. Like his father, he had believed that the Declaratory Act was a meaningless gesture. Now, however, Parliament had "rekindled the Flame," giving radical leaders another opportunity to stir up colonial opposition.[13] William also insisted that sending troops to Boston was a huge mistake. Soldiers might be able to secure outward obedience to the law, he conceded, but they would never change people's beliefs. "Men's Minds are sour'd," he maintained, and there was "no Force on Earth" that would "make the Assemblies acknowledge by any Act of theirs that the Parliament has a Right to impose Taxes on America." If William did not say that he agreed with this position, neither did he condemn it.[14]

It is tempting to wonder what would have happened had Hillsborough demanded William Franklin's resignation in 1768. William would surely have had no reason to remain loyal to a government that had rejected his services and questioned his loyalty. Had he been unable to secure another royal post, he may well have ended up supporting the Patriot cause. Instead, he kept his job. Four years later, when Hillsborough was forced to resign, he and Benjamin rejoiced. And if William did not get a better job or a heftier salary after 1772, neither did he worry anymore about losing his governorship. His father had taught him that authority was generally benign. Both men could agree that, while it sometimes took a while, the English government eventually came to its senses. Thus, they continued to support the king and defend the colonies.

It took William Franklin longer than it did most colonial governors to realize that he would have to choose between obeying the king and serving New Jersey. Like Benjamin, he had gotten his political start defending the rights of the Pennsylvania Assembly against the claims of the Proprietors. And so long as he remained in New Jersey he sought a balance between the governor and the House, never denying that the "democratical" part of government needed to be preserved.

William, after all, was not just a colonial governor. Like Thomas Hutchinson, he was an American. He sincerely believed that he could uphold the king's prerogatives while he protected the colonists' rights. He never changed his mind. Indeed, as the differences between England and the colonies heightened, he always argued that the problems roiling the Empire could be solved by closer relationships and better communication. He continued to champion the plan for colonial representation in Parliament that both his father and Massachusetts Governor Bernard had once advocated. He also called for the creation of a Crown commission in the colonies composed of governors like himself and assisted by "some Gentlemen of Abilities Moderation and Candour from Great Britain" that could forge a compromise that reasonable men on both sides of the Atlantic would find acceptable.[15] Significantly, he counted on his own father to help him find a basis for reconciliation.

Nor, of course, was he totally wrong to do so. William had, after all, gained his longing for a united Empire from his father, and the lessons he learned early on stuck with him long after the colonies declared their independence. He knew, moreover, that Benjamin had no desire to see the Empire torn asunder. The elder Franklin's quarrel with London had almost invariably been with Parliament, occasionally with the king's ministers, but not, until the very end, with the king himself. In 1766, Benjamin had actually proposed that America and Great Britain be unified along the lines of Scotland and England. Admittedly, especially after 1770, Benjamin seemed more concerned with promoting the rights of the colonies than he did in defending the prerogatives of the king. But while he grew increasingly pessimistic about the possibility of securing a rapprochement, he did not stop trying to effect a reconciliation. His decision to send the Hutchinson/Oliver letters to Massachusetts had been reached with that goal in mind.

The rupture between Benjamin and William Franklin came gradually, virtually imperceptibly. In that respect, it mirrored the movement toward independence as a whole. No one event, no particular disagreement was enough in itself to lead father and son, colonies and England to go their separate ways. Even in the days immediately preceding the Cockpit, Benjamin's views were ambiguous enough to assure William that their own differences were mere matters of degree. In 1773

Benjamin had appeared almost conciliatory, remarking that William was a "true government man, which I do not wonder at, nor do I aim at converting you." He asked only that his son act "uprightly and steadily," leaving all New Jersey inhabitants "happier than you found them." If you do that, he predicted, "whatever your political principles are, your memory will be honored."[16] After the Cockpit, Benjamin was less tolerant. Although he, himself, had once urged Bostonians to pay for the tea they had so unceremoniously dumped into the harbor, he was disdainful when William suggested exactly the same thing. "I do not, as much as you do," he observed, "wonder that the Massachusetts have not offered Payment for the Tea." But you, he continued, "who are a thorough Courtier, see every thing with Government Eyes."[17]

If there was a single turning-point in the relationship between father and son, it came in the wake of Benjamin's revelation that it was he who had sent the Hutchinson/Oliver letters to the Bay Colony. When William first heard about the letters, he had written to Benjamin describing Hutchinson's "gloomy and low spirited" mood.[18] He was aware of the rumors floating around the colonies to the effect that his father was responsible for Hutchinson's plight, but he dismissed them as preposterous. As he had done during the Stamp Act crisis, he defended Benjamin against such accusations. Wouldn't his father have confided in him if the gossips were right? Hadn't both men complained bitterly when they suspected that London officials had intercepted their own mail, looking for evidence of disloyalty? Although he, himself, had occasionally criticized Hutchinson, convinced that he was prone to pick unnecessary quarrels with the Massachusetts Assembly, William clearly sympathized with a fellow governor whose privacy had been so callously violated. He simply assumed that his father would feel the same way. Thus, he was stunned when he read Benjamin's letter, written on September 1, 1773, which almost casually admitted that he was, indeed, the source of the "famous Boston letters."[19] He was even more bewildered when his father airily dismissed his concerns for Hutchinson's emotional well-being. "I don't wonder that Hutchinson should be dejected," Benjamin remarked. "It must be an uncomfortable thing to live among people who he is conscious universally detest him." But, he added gratuitously, if the governor thought he would be welcome in England, he was sadly mistaken. No one in London approved of his conduct, either.[20]

Both Franklins quickly backed away from what could easily have become an open conflict. Although they must have recognized at some level that their views of imperial affairs were diverging, neither would admit it, not to himself, not to the other. Thus, although Benjamin berated his son for his inability to appreciate the "heinous" nature of Hutchinson's letters, he rushed to find an explanation for William's perspective. "Perhaps," he said, "you had not read them all, nor perhaps the council's remarks on them."[21] And he continued to hope that his own powers of persuasion, not to mention the ties of affection that still bound the two men, would eventually do their magic, persuading William to reconsider his determination to hang on to his governorship.

William, too, refused to believe that he and his father were drifting apart. He did not see that while his own views had not changed, his father's perspective had undergone a profound transformation. Even after Benjamin's part in the affair of the letters became public knowledge, even after the hearing at the Cockpit, William chose to ignore what from hindsight appears to have been obvious. To the contrary, he pinned his hopes on Benjamin's return—always promised, always postponed, but now more likely—to America. If Benjamin would just come home, thought William, he would see what was apparently invisible to him from his position in London. He would surely acknowledge that the colonies were out of control and veering toward anarchy. They were meeting in extralegal conclaves, making and enforcing laws that had no legitimacy, destroying the delicate balance between power and liberty. Once Benjamin arrived in Philadelphia he would frame "some Plan for Accommodation of our Differences that would [meet] with the Approbation of a Majority of the Delegates" at another meeting.[22] William remained convinced that the colonists longed for such a plan. If Benjamin was certain that most Englishmen disapproved of their government's treatment of its colonies, so William believed that the bulk of Americans despised those radicals who had somehow contrived to seize the reins of power, ignoring the wishes of the moderate majority. "Few," he explained, "have the Courage to declare their Disapprobation publickly, as they well know, if they do not conform, they are in Danger of becoming Objects of popular Resentment."[23]

Benjamin did come home, of course, and he spent much of his time on the return voyage writing a detailed account of his experiences in the year after his humiliation at the Cockpit. He addressed his missive to his son. If William thought he could convince his father of the error of his ways, Benjamin was confident that he could persuade William to abandon his loyalty to the king. His letter was a last-ditch effort to impress upon his son the depth of his own hostility to a ministry whose every action reflected its determination to destroy colonial rights. He must have known, however, that his efforts would prove futile. When he arrived in America, Benjamin went immediately to Philadelphia. There would have been a time, not so very long ago, when he would have rushed to the New Jersey capital, eager to embrace a beloved son whom he had not laid eyes on in over a decade. Now, however, he thought it just as well that he wait.

The two men finally had their reunion, meeting at Trevose, Galloway's grand estate in Bucks County, Pennsylvania. Both Franklins, by their actions, had already taken sides. Blood had been shed at Lexington and Concord, and the Second Continental Congress was meeting in Philadelphia. Benjamin was a member of that Congress, while William opposed the very existence of what he saw as an illegal gathering and was actively trying to undermine it. Acting as a self-appointed spy, he was regularly sending secret intelligence to London. His letters were filled with information he had gleaned from men who had no idea that their private conversations with the governor would end up in Dartmouth's hands. He was, in other words, doing exactly what Thomas Hutchinson had once done, behaving in the very way that Benjamin Franklin had found so "heinous."

As the two Franklins greeted their host and awkwardly embraced, they talked of trivialities before getting down to serious business. Benjamin and William had avoided political discussions of late, and thus they didn't know quite how to begin. Galloway, once Benjamin's protégé, confidant, and his most valuable partner in the campaign for royal government, was even more uncomfortable. He had made his unhappiness with colonial affairs abundantly clear when he refused to serve as a delegate to the Second Continental Congress. Still, as the Madeira began to flow, the three men loosened up, reminiscing about the good times they once had shared, perhaps talking about their visions for the future. By the end of the long evening, William and Benjamin realized what Galloway probably already knew. There was no basis for an accommodation of their differences. William acknowledged that his father no longer had a desire to broker a peace between England and the colonies. Benjamin realized that William intended to remain loyal to the king. Thus, Galloway remained at Trevose, Benjamin rode back to Philadelphia, and William left for New Jersey.

Neither father nor son should have been surprised at the views of the other. In essence, their perspectives were the product of their very different experiences over the years. Benjamin was still smarting from his ordeal at the Cockpit, and he was truly alienated from a government he had once longed to join. He disdained "the total Ignorance," the "Prejudice and Passion," the "willful Perversion of Plain Truth" that he had seen firsthand during his final days in London. Parliament's behavior, he said, made its "Claim of Sovereignty over three millions of virtuous sensible People in America, seem the greatest of Absurdities, since they appear'd to have scarce Discretion enough to govern a Herd of Swine."[24] William was taken aback by such vitriol. If his father had been mocked by the men at the Cockpit, he had been maligned by New Jersey's lawmakers. He had suffered humiliation from the very "virtuous and sensible People" whom his father idolized but did not know. While he had once enjoyed good relations with his assembly, by 1770 he was finding it difficult to forge a consensus on big issues or small. Everything was a contest, and in each instance the level of trust on both sides declined. William could tell his tales of ambitious and selfish colonists who would employ any means to destroy the Empire so that they could gain power for themselves. "However mad you may think the Measures of the Ministry are," he bristled, "yet I trust you have Candor enough to acknowledge that we are no ways behind hand with them in In[stances] of Madness on this Side the Water."[25] Benjamin distrusted the motives of English leaders; his son was equally convinced that colonial malcontents were responsible for what looked to him like a disaster. Benjamin was positive that the balance between liberty and power had tipped dangerously toward power; William knew that in the colonies, democracy was in the ascendancy.

The long and fruitful friendship between Joseph Galloway and Benjamin Franklin ended at Trevose. The relationship between Benjamin and William dissolved more slowly but just as inexorably. Father and son still corresponded on occasion, although they seldom discussed politics. Benjamin and his sister Jane stopped by the governor's mansion in November 1775. They chatted for a bit, ate dinner with

William and his wife, but did not stay the night. Both Franklins were probably relieved when Benjamin announced that the press of business necessitated his immediate return to Philadelphia. He made no effort to discuss the nature of the affairs that called him back. Father and son did not meet again until after the war.

The time when it was possible for any American to serve two masters was nearing an end. While some colonists tried to remain neutral, such a course was not an option for Benjamin or William Franklin. Although each man fervently hoped that the other would sit quietly on the sidelines, neither was capable of withdrawing from the fray. William strove valiantly to persuade New Jersey's assembly to chart its own, moderate course rather than following the instructions of an illegal Continental Congress—a Congress in which his own father was playing a leading role. And he came as close as any royal governor to achieving his ends. Whenever he convened his assembly he begged its members to ignore Congress and maintain their own relationship with England. He continued to insist—and perhaps even to believe—that while few if any in New Jersey would "draw their Swords in Support of Taxation," there were many, probably a majority, who would "fight to preserve the Supremacy of Parliament in other respects" and who would surely want to preserve America's "Connexion with Great Britain."[26] He never for a moment thought that the colony's rights would be endangered by a continued loyalty to the Crown. To the contrary, he lectured New Jersey lawmakers, you have before you "two Roads—one evidently leading to Peace, Happiness and a Restoration of the publick Tranquility—the other inevitably conducting you to Anarchy, Misery and the Horrors of a Civil War."[27] While he left no doubt which option he preferred, he knew that the legislators would disagree. And of course he was right.

　　While William struggled to keep his old government from disintegrating, Benjamin began to lay the foundations for a new one. The elder Franklin was everywhere doing everything. The Pennsylvania Assembly appointed him as a delegate to the Second Continental Congress almost as soon as he arrived on American shores. He was soon hard at work helping raise men and supplies in preparation for possible hostilities. He was up every day at six, and he seldom retired before nightfall. Although his schedule was exhausting, it was also exhilarating. No longer trying to mediate between increasingly divergent perspectives, Franklin no doubt relished his newfound single-minded commitment to independence. At long last he could talk freely of England's "barbarous Tyranny" and its "mad Measures."[28] And he insisted that separation from England was "inevitable."[29] If he was frustrated by anything, it was the need to proceed with caution as he was fully aware that not all delegates at the Continental Congress were ready to sever their ties with England. His old nemesis, John Dickinson, was only one member of his own Pennsylvania delegation who was fighting steadily against those like Franklin who had long given up on rapprochement.

For William, the end—of his relationship to both his father and New Jersey—was near. He was losing control of his colony and he knew it. He was fully aware that royal governors elsewhere were already abandoning their posts, fleeing before they could be attacked by colonial firebrands. Still, although he feared that he might be captured by his enemies and led "like a Bear through the Country," he refused to abandon his post, determined to serve as a symbolic reminder that legitimate government in the colonies had not disappeared everywhere.[30] Thus he continued to send his little "secret and confidential" packets of information to Lord Dartmouth, relishing the favor in which he was held by the secretary at a time when he felt as though everyone in the colonies was against him. If most people in New Jersey now saw him as an embarrassing obstacle to their aims, he finally enjoyed the undiluted support of the government at home.

In January 1776, William Franklin sent another packet to Lord Dartmouth. As usual it was bristling with newspapers and documents that he hoped would help the secretary gauge the colonial mood. Unfortunately for him, his packet never reached England. Instead, it was intercepted by William Alexander, once one of William's closest friends, now a leader of the opposition. The timing could not have been worse. The Continental Congress had just ordered the colonies to disarm and incarcerate all Americans who refused to pledge their loyalty to the self-styled government in Philadelphia. Thus, Alexander thought he was doing his duty when he sent one hundred soldiers to the governor's mansion to arrest William Franklin. On this occasion, William obtained a reprieve. New

Jersey Chief Justice Frederick Smyth intervened and for the moment, he remained a free man.

There were many who hoped that the governor would use his freedom to quit the colony, thus saving them the trouble and embarrassment of dealing with a man who was clearly a thorn in their side. But, despite his growing sense of isolation, William refused to oblige them. Although he was angry and a little afraid, he found his predicament something of a relief. Just as Benjamin had been liberated once he arrived in America and had no further obligation to mediate between England and its colonies, so William, once he realized that there was no point in battling for the hearts and minds of New Jersey's inhabitants, was free to lash out at the very colonists whose allegiance he had tried to secure for so long. He worried, of course, about his wife, Elizabeth, who, with no "relations or connexions" to comfort her, was prostrate, the "least sudden Noise almost throws her into Hysterics."[31] But for himself, he simply dug in his heels and waited.

William Franklin's career as governor of New Jersey unraveled completely in the spring of 1776. His father was on the road to Montreal, part of a delegation intent upon persuading Canadians to join forces with their neighbor to the south. It was a wasted effort, but one that spared him the anguish he no doubt would have felt as Congress set in motion the events that resulted in William's imprisonment. On May 15, Congress instructed the colonies to abandon their governments and form new ones, in essence putting an end to the old provincial regimes. Two weeks later, William Franklin defied the congressional resolution, ordering his assembly to convene in New Jersey's capital. The governor's enemies immediately swung into action. They called upon all lawmakers to ignore Franklin's summons, and the next day New Jersey's newly formed Provincial Congress announced that the governor's attempt to meet with the legislature in direct violation of a congressional order had made him "an enemy to the liberties of this country."[32] Thus they prepared to arrest William Franklin. They still hoped that they would not have to incarcerate the governor, promising him that if he would only give his word not to interfere in their activities, they would allow him to retire to his farm on Rancocas Creek where he could live out his days in peace. But if they thought William would accept their offer, they were sadly mistaken.

William refused even to negotiate with his captors. He did not recognize their authority nor did he think he was an enemy to New Jersey's liberties. All he had done was to ask duly elected legislators to do their job. As far as he was concerned, it was New Jersey's Provincial Congress that was denying the colony the right to be ruled by its own representatives. It was he who was trying to maintain a balance between liberty and power, recognizing the need to preserve every branch of government. If the Provincial Congress had its way, he predicted, democratic tyranny, the "most debasing of all possible Tyrannies," would be the result. "Depend upon it," he warned, "you can never place yourselves in a happier situation than in your ancient constitutional dependency on Great Britain. No Independent State ever was or ever can be happy as we have been, and might still be, under that government."[33] Whether he was right or wrong was irrelevant. The men who were now in charge of New Jersey's future had had enough. When they asked the Continental Congress for permission to arrest the governor, Congress, no doubt glad that Benjamin Franklin was out of town, responded in the affirmative. On June, 19, 1776, William's carriage rolled away from the governor's mansion, surrounded by sixteen armed guards. As William kissed Elizabeth goodbye, he had no idea that he would not see his wife again.

William's interrogation began on June 21. But it might as well never have taken place. The governor refused to answer even the simplest questions, believing that doing so would legitimate an illegal process. Like his father at the Cockpit, he remained silent, contemptuous of the men who now held the upper hand. Just as Benjamin had endured the bombastic and sarcastic invective of Alexander Wedderburn, so did William suffer the calumny of John Witherspoon, president of the College of New Jersey. Witherspoon mocked William's fine airs and his pretensions to gentility, reminding everyone that the governor was nothing more than a base-born bastard. Once Witherspoon's venom was spent, Franklin's captors led the governor from the room. They quickly decided, with no dissenting voice to be heard, that William Franklin, governor of New Jersey for thirteen years, was a "virulent enemy to this country" and they asked the Continental Congress to designate some place for his confinement.[34] Congress alertly complied. Franklin would be moved to Connecticut where Governor Jonathan Trumbull would take him into custody.

On July 4, 1776, eight days after his little caravan left Burlington, William Franklin rode into the Connecticut capital. Even as he traveled toward Hartford, his father was back in Philadelphia, a member of the committee that was drafting what became known as the Declaration of Independence. Although he was fully aware of what was happening to his son, Benjamin did not lift a finger on William's behalf. He was already preparing to help win the independence that the Continental Congress had declared. He would soon travel to France where he would help forge an American-French alliance that was instrumental, even crucial, to the new nation's military success.

William's future was not so rosy. He remained in Connecticut for two years, first in Wallingford and then in Middletown where he was accorded the relative freedom generally offered to gentlemen prisoners. But when Congress discovered that he was violating his trust, making every effort to sabotage the independence movement, it sent him to Litchfield, where he remained in solitary confinement for eight months. His lodgings were cramped and dirty. His captors even denied him the use of pen and paper. He was virtually cut off from the outside world. Elizabeth wrote to her father-in-law, begging for help meeting her basic expenses, and pleading with him to intervene on behalf of his only living son. Franklin sent her a little money, curtly reminding her that others were suffering much more than she. He completely ignored her references to William's predicament. Elizabeth finally fled New Jersey in the spring of 1777, escaping to New York just ahead of advancing American troops. She survived the move, but died almost as soon as her journey ended.

William finally emerged from his Litchfield jail in October 1778, the beneficiary of a prisoner exchange arranged by the Continental Congress. Bitter, emaciated, determined to destroy those whom he blamed for the death of his wife and his own loss of honor and position, he went immediately to New York City, then in the hands of General Henry Clinton, commander of His Majesty's forces. There he became the president of the Board of Associated Loyalists, a paramilitary outfit that organized and equipped loyalist soldiers and executed guerilla raids on patriot strongholds. In that capacity, he became more aware than ever of the terrible sufferings of many loyalists. William was by no means the only American to be imprisoned under the authority of the Continental Congress. But even those loyalists who remained free did not emerge unscathed. Individual state legislatures confiscated their possessions. Franklin's friend, Joseph Galloway, for instance, was stripped of all of his property. Thomas Hutchinson lost his Milton residence and all its furnishings. Even more insulting to the Massachusetts governor, rumor had it that marauders had stabbed his portrait with bayonets and that George Washington was using Hutchinson's coach to ride about the New England countryside. Some— teachers and lawyers in particular—lost their jobs. They were prohibited from serving on juries, from voting, or from traveling more than a mile from their homes. Many ended their lives in exile, far from a country they continued to love, even if they deplored the course that it had taken.

Civil wars are often the most vicious wars. Thus, not surprisingly, the war for independence led Americans on both sides to commit atrocities and acts of cruelty that were barbaric even by the standard of the times. When the Continental forces and the king's army faced one another on the field of battle, they tended—generally if not always—to play by the rules. There were no rules however, when neighbor fought neighbor, each convinced that the other was betraying the values that should have held the community together. Battles pitting American against American occurred in every state. The backcountry of North and South Carolina was the scene of "social anarchy," where "murder and banditry, brutal intimidation, and retaliation became a way of life."[35] In Pennsylvania, authorities viewed Quakers with mistrust, even though the Friends tried to remain strictly neutral. Both in New York and in eastern New Jersey, fratricidal conflict was particularly brutal. Each side could tell gruesome tales of a virtual state of nature, where homes were invaded and demolished and friends and neighbors were dismembered, tortured, and killed.

As president of the Associated Board of Loyalists, William Franklin himself—once the fierce opponent of vigilante action—authorized what in today's world would be characterized as "terrorist activity." Especially after Cornwallis's defeat at Yorktown in 1781, loyalists were desperate. Watching as the victory they had once thought was theirs for the taking slip away, they tried to provoke George Washington to retaliate against them, thus keeping the war going as long as possible. Thus William authorized the lynching of New Jersey Patriot Joshua Huddy. Huddy was known for his part in atrocities that had taken the lives and limbs of many loyalists. Franklin and his supporters no doubt thought he had earned his ignominious end. The aftermath of the incident, however, was hardly what the former governor had hoped for. When George Washington began calling for William's head, the British, who saw Franklin as a nuisance and an embarrassment, were not eager to defend him. Realizing that whatever small influence he may have had was now nonexistent, William fled New York for the safety and comfort of London. He never quite shook off the damage to his reputation that resulted from his involvement in the Huddy affair. And it was probably more responsible than anything for his father's anger, making it impossible for the two men ever to bridge the chasm that divided them.

After Yorktown, the war was virtually over. Lord North enjoyed Benjamin Franklin's discomfort at the Cockpit less than a decade earlier. Franklin was triumphant in the end. North resigned his position. Negotiations began that would eventually result in England's recognition of American independence—negotiations in which Benjamin took a leading role. Significantly, he, more than any other American at the table, fought hard against the British request that the new American government compensate former loyalists for the property they lost during the war.

Many of those who took different sides during the war managed to bury their differences when hostilities ceased. The Franklins were not so fortunate. While Benjamin celebrated American independence and returned triumphant to Philadelphia, his son lived the rest of his life in exile. When the war officially ended in 1783, William reached out to his father, hoping that their own private war might be over as well. Believing that the time had come to let bygones be bygones, he wrote to Benjamin, hoping, he said, to "revive that affectionate Intercourse and Connection which till the Commencement of the late Troubles has been the Pride and Happiness of my Life." He refused to apologize for his loyalism. "I uniformly acted from a Strong Sense of what I conceived my Duty to my King and Regard to my Country," he insisted. "If I have been mistaken, I cannot help it. It is an Error of Judgment that the maturist reflection I am capable of cannot rectify, and I verily believe were the same Circumstances to occur Tomorrow, my Conduct would be exactly similar to what it was heretofore." He nevertheless asked his father for a "personal interview," imagining that now that he had "broken the ice," the two men might be friends once more.[36]

Although he had chosen the winning side, Benjamin Franklin seemed determined to play the victim. He had lost many friends due to the war. He had once sympathized with Thomas Hutchinson. He had valued his relationship with Joseph Galloway almost until the end. He could remember many other Americans with whom he had once been close, who had ended up supporting king and country. While he regretted the necessity to sever his ties with men whose friendship he once had valued, his rupture with his son was the most painful of all. "Nothing," he wrote William, "has hurt me so much and affected me with such keen Sensations as to find myself deserted in my old Age by my only Son; and not only deserted, but to find him taking up Arms against me in a Cause wherein my good Fame, Fortune and Life were all at Stake."[37] To the very end, the elder Franklin valued his reputation. Just as he had once resented his very public humiliation by Alexander Wedderburn at the Cockpit, so he was mortified by his son's open support of the king. Had William remained neutral, Benjamin may have forgiven him. But he had refused to do so.

Father and son met just once after the war. In 1785 Benjamin was setting sail for home. He stopped briefly at Southampton, and William traveled to the port town to bid him adieu. Their encounter was brief, businesslike, and not especially happy. Benjamin convinced William to sell his New Jersey lands to Temple Franklin for a paltry sum. He also demanded some of his son's New York property in exchange for a debt of fifteen hundred pounds. That taken care of, Benjamin curtly said his farewells and crossed the Atlantic for the last time. He lived for five more years, serving as the oldest delegate by far to the Constitutional Convention, greeting a stream of well-wishers who wanted to see him one more time before he died. He never forgave his son. His will left William some worthless Nova Scotia lands as well as the books and papers that he already had in his possession. "The part he acted against me in the late War," Benjamin tersely explained, "which is of public Notoriety, will account for my leaving him no more of an Estate he endeavored to deprive me of."[38]

William never returned to America. He remained in London, performing numerous services great and small for his fellow exiles. He married again, in 1788, but when his wife Mary died twenty-three years later, he was more alone than ever. He reestablished contact with Temple, but the two were virtual strangers and did not really get along. While his son had inherited the Franklin charm, he did not seem to have many of his progenitors' virtues. Something of a dilettante and a bit of a wastrel, he flitted from project to project, never settling down to finish any of them. When he fathered an illegitimate daughter, Ellen, it was William, not Temple, who took Ellen into his home and raised her as his own. Long after Benjamin died, William still looked fondly upon his father, reminiscing about the good times they had shared, conveniently forgetting the bad. He often remarked that Ellen bore a marked resemblance to Benjamin. He also began to contemplate writing his father's biography. But when he died, in 1814, he had yet to begin his project in earnest.

Benjamin and William Franklin had begun their political lives as Empire men. Neither saw any conflict between their desire to defend American liberties and their attempt to bring the colonies ever closer to king and country. In that regard, father and son reflected the views of virtually all of His Majesty's mainland subjects at midcentury. Even as tensions between England and America grew deeper, the Franklins, along with most other colonists, clung to their vision of a united Empire. It was only after his humiliation at the Cockpit that Benjamin Franklin finally conceded that his valiant efforts over the years had been in vain. For his part, William was not blind to Parliament's mistakes. He understood, even agreed with, the colonists' frustrations with English policy. He, too, thought the Stamp Act was probably unconstitutional and surely ill-advised; he disapproved of the Townshend Duties; he was unhappy when Lord Hillsborough sent troops to Boston in 1768. He loved America, especially his adopted colony of New Jersey. He truly believed that the colonies would be helpless without English support and was convinced that a country without a monarch would inevitably descend into chaos.

Historians often wonder why William—and the countless other colonists who shared his perspective—"decided" to remain loyal to England. In most ways, however, that is the wrong question to ask. The loyalists did not "decide" anything. They simply remained where they were. They did not—for whatever reason, they could not—change.

They were comfortable enough with the ways and relationships of the past. They feared an uncharted future. It was the Patriots—men like Benjamin Franklin—who changed, who abandoned their old loyalties in favor of new ones, who were willing to take an incredible risk—a risk that could easily end in disaster for themselves and for the colonies they loved. They might, after all, fail to win independence. Even if they won, they could find that William Franklin was right, that they were not capable of self-government. They would be ripe for invasion by Europeans interested in expanding their holdings in the western hemisphere. They could easily fall to fighting among themselves, condemning their children and grandchildren to a life of perpetual war. Nevertheless, they made a leap of faith. They declared their independence, not with joy but with sadness as they turned their back on a country they had once loved but could no longer tolerate. They also made enemies of friends, neighbors, and family members whom they could not persuade to support their cause.

In July 1776, just days after Congress had declared independence, Benjamin Franklin met briefly with Admiral Richard Howe, commander of the British naval forces. Howe had come to America with a last-ditch offer to the Continental Congress. England would grant Americans everything they wanted—except for independence. Such a concession may have been acceptable to the colonists at one time, but not any more. As he informed Howe that Congress had rejected his olive branch, Franklin grew philosophical. He had, he pointed out, always labored to "preserve from breaking, that fine and noble China Vase the British Empire: for I knew that being once broken, the separate Parts could not retain even their Share of the Strength or Value that existed in the Whole."[39] Now, however, that china vase was shattered. The Empire was dissolving. The relationship between Benjamin and William Franklin was at an end, as well.

Epilogue: The Meaning of the Cockpit

His humiliation at the Cockpit was truly a critical encounter for Benjamin Franklin. Had his ordeal not occurred when and how it did, he may have remained in England after 1775, still haunting Whitehall's corridors, talking, cajoling, offering one proposal after another, doing his best to keep the Empire together. He would probably not have been in a hurry to leave London. He had resided there for nearly a decade. Deborah had died, as had many of his Philadelphia friends. He often remarked that were he to return home he would know no one there. He would be a stranger among strangers. Moreover, he had forged deep friendships over the years with men and women in London and its environs, and could easily imagine living comfortably there forever. To complicate matters, many of his remaining close emotional bonds were often as not with men like his son William and Joseph Galloway, both of whom remained loyal to the king.

True enough, Franklin may well have become a "Patriot" in any event. He had, after all, suffered innumerable personal setbacks in recent years, and he had been rebuffed all too many times during his final sojourn in England. Moreover, his service as the Massachusetts agent had made him especially sensitive to parliamentary encroachments on colonial "rights." After the Tea Party, England's hardliners were more in control than ever and the opportunities for the kinds of compromises that Franklin valued were fewer. Thus, if the colonists had decided to make a clean break from the British Empire in 1776, Franklin may well have left for home. If he had done so, however, he would have joined the forces of rebellion with genuine sorrow. He would not have done so as England's angry and implacable foe. He may not have been one of the most determined of Patriots, relentlessly pressing the members of the Second Continental Congress to declare their independence sooner rather than later. And if he returned as a reluctant revolutionary, he may not have gained the trust of those colonists who were at the forefront of the fight. He may not have been a member of the committee that drafted the Declaration of Independence. More importantly, his appointment as the leading member of the new nation's diplomatic mission to France would have encountered serious opposition from Congress's radical contingent. Alexander Wedderburn had called Benjamin Franklin a true "incendiary." At the time he made that accusation, the solicitor was wrong. But the experience at the Cockpit had turned a moderate into a radical, a still-loyal Englishman into an angry patriot. And thus, despite his age and his lowly beginnings, Franklin was a central figure in America's fight for independence.

The Cockpit incident altered Franklin's vision. He had once dismissed the fears of colonists who were convinced that the king's ministers were the masterminds of an insidious plot to destroy liberty everywhere. Franklin characterized those apprehensions as unduly paranoid, the product of a mindset that saw the world in black and white, that could not comprehend the complexities with which real men in the real world grappled every day. After January 1774 Franklin was much more likely to see what popular leaders like Samuel Adams and Patrick Henry had been describing for a decade or more. While he still clung to his belief that most Englishmen sympathized with the colonies, he was forced to concede that the men who held the reins of power viewed Americans—even talented Americans like himself— with barely disguised disdain. If someone like Wedderburn could sneer at him, a world-renowned scientist and man of letters, what must his adversary think of ordinary colonists? If ministers who once thought he deserved a government sinecure now laughed gleefully at Wedderburn's gibes, how could Franklin cling to the belief that Englishmen would ever join their colonial counterparts in an effort to create a pan-Atlantic empire that would be the envy of the world?

The Cockpit incident also forced Franklin to recognize just how much his own views had diverged from men like his son. When he heard about his father's humiliation at the Cockpit, William Franklin did not offer Benjamin much in the way of sympathy. Nor did he consider resigning his governorship in protest, even though Benjamin clearly wanted him to do so. There had been a time when William and Benjamin Franklin had shared everything. Proud Americans, proud Englishmen, loyal subjects of a young and promising king, neither could envision a time when they would have to choose between loyalty to their principles and loyalty to one another. In 1763 the Franklins were like all Americans, convinced that their well-being rested upon a strong connection to the mother country. In a little over a decade, that perspective no longer existed for most colonists. Indeed, they had decided that England would not rest easy until it had destroyed their liberties and placed them in a position of helpless subjugation.

Still, there remained a sizeable minority who continued to reject the very idea that government officials were involved in an insidious plot to enslave the colonies. While they disliked the Stamp Act, the Townshend Duties, and the Tea Act as much as the Patriots did, they saw each effort to tax the colonies as a discrete, unrelated decision and an honest mistake, not as evidence of a diabolical scheme to shred what was left of the "rights of Englishmen" in His Majesty's mainland possessions. Thus, when the members of the Second Continental Congress voted to declare their independence from England, men like William Franklin, Joseph Galloway, and Thomas Hutchinson were horrified, convinced that the colonies they loved had made a decision they would soon regret. That decision did not just set the colonists against England; it set colonists against one another.

The Cockpit changed Benjamin Franklin, pushing him toward a decision that he had been trying with increasing difficulty to avoid. That being the case, it seems only fair to ask what, if anything, would have been different—for Franklin and for the colonists—had events played out differently. Counterfactual history is not fashionable, and generally speaking it is not very useful. What point is there, after all, in asking what "might have been," when clearly what happened *did* happen and nothing can change that reality? Nevertheless, if we are to think of history in terms of "critical encounters," then we must at least wonder what actually changed because of an event that occurred at one particular point in time. It seems reasonable to contend that independence would have been declared and eventually won no matter what happened to Franklin personally. But as Franklin's experience surely indicates, there were many moments between 1765 and 1776 when leaders on either side of the Atlantic might have acted differently, hence avoiding—or at least postponing—the conflict between England and its colonies. Real people living in their own world, facing their own problems, do make choices. And if those choices and their consequences seem obvious, almost inevitable now, they by no means seemed so simple or clear to the men and women who actually made them. For eighteenth-century Englishmen and colonists, the future was not a foregone conclusion. It was open-ended and full of possibilities.

Benjamin Franklin, no matter what Wedderburn said to the contrary, was no incendiary. He enjoyed the friendship of future loyalists as well as of future patriots. His support for independence was not inevitable. He assumed that he could effect a reconciliation between England and its colonies. Had it not been for his humiliation at the Cockpit, he may not have abandoned his quest for unity quite so soon. It seems safe to say, moreover, that the Cockpit incident could have played out differently or been avoided altogether. Consider the alternative scenarios—none of which is especially far-fetched. Would, for instance, Franklin's stance have been different had he succeeded in gaining a royal sinecure, one that he steadily sought, occasionally thought was within his grasp, and always believed he deserved? Or what if the timing of his appearance at the Cockpit had been different? Franklin had admitted publicly that he was responsible for the controversy over the Hutchinson/Oliver correspondence on December 24, 1773—less than a month before his appearance at the Cockpit. He might easily have made this admission much earlier, thus giving observers an opportunity to let their tempers cool. Or he could have waited until after his appearance before the Privy Council to make his part in the affair known, making it difficult for Wedderburn to argue that Franklin bore the primary responsibility for the enmity between the Massachusetts Assembly and Governor Hutchinson. Or when he learned that Hutchinson's agent had asked Wedderburn to represent him before the Privy Council, Franklin could have elected not to ask for more time to secure his own lawyer. Had that happened, the hearing would have taken place before news of the Tea Party arrived in London. The council would still have rejected the Massachusetts petition. But the entire matter would have been the routine affair that Franklin had expected it to be. The councilors would have been less likely to laugh at Wedderburn's vicious diatribe, and Franklin would have left the Cockpit with the sense that he had been treated fairly even if Massachusetts had lost its case.

Franklin eventually may have come to the conclusion that independence was necessary. But at least until 1774, he—like most patriotic Americans—did not see Anglo-American relationships as irrevocably broken. If his treatment at the Cockpit was avoidable, perhaps the American Revolution was not inevitable either. Franklin always insisted that the English government missed a number of golden opportunities to reconcile its differences with the colonies. Parliament might, for example, have listened to Edmund Burke, refusing to act upon its right to tax the colonies after 1766, thus removing the central bone of contention that so troubled principled men on both sides of the Atlantic. Or Lord North could have heeded the advice of those who thought he should use the Tea Act as an excuse to remove the tax on imported tea. Without the tea tax, the Boston Tea Party, of course, would never have occurred nor would Parliament have found it necessary to pass the Coercive Acts. The government could even have followed the advice of both Governor Francis Bernard and Benjamin Franklin, offering the colonists representation in Parliament, destroying in one decisive move the Americans' claim that they were being taxed without representation. And what would have happened if government officials had reacted to the revelations surrounding the Hutchinson/Oliver correspondence as Franklin had thought that they would—making scapegoats of both men, thus defusing rather than escalating tensions?

It may well be that the Revolution was inevitable, even if people at the time did not believe that this was so. Decisions that seem logical in hindsight were in many cases politically impossible to make. Given its own history, given its fears that Americans were conspiring to achieve independence, Parliament was simply not prepared to back down in the face of what it saw as colonial intransigence. Americans who were both proud of their English heritage and determined to preserve their rights as Englishmen found it almost unthinkable to submit to what appeared to be the ministry's desire to enslave them. With or without Franklin's support, they would have eventually declared and even won their independence. No one person—even Franklin—was, after all, indispensable. To be sure, it is doubtful that the Continental Congress could have found a legate as adept as Benjamin Franklin to negotiate a military alliance with France once the war for independence began. Franklin was a celebrated intellectual and a shrewd diplomat, the likes of which the world has seldom seen. Still, the desire to make life as difficult for England as possible was probably reason enough to lead France to join the American cause, and France may have entered the fray without Franklin's prodding.

If America could have survived without Franklin, Franklin would not have done so well without America. He made more than his fair share of political mistakes over the years. He advocated a royal government for Pennsylvania at the very time when Anglo-colonial relationships were taking a turn for the worse. He did not appreciate the depth of American antipathy to the Stamp Act or even the Townshend Duties as quickly as he could have and should have. His own testimony before Parliament bolstered Charles Townshend's belief that the colonies would accept an "external tax," and thus the Chancellor of the Exchequer felt especially betrayed when Americans rejected his taxes, seemingly changing the rules of the game to suit their own selfish ends. And of course, Franklin sent the Hutchinson/Oliver letters to Massachusetts in a misguided effort to bring England and its colonies closer together. In the end, however, Benjamin Franklin made one decision that allowed most observers then and especially now to forget all of his other errata. He embraced independence, and found himself on the winning side of the war between England and its colonies. In doing so, he preserved a special place for himself as one of the most valuable members of the new nation's founding generation.

NOTES

....

Chapter 1

1. Benjamin Franklin (hereafter BF) to Thomas Cushing, February 15, 1774, in Leonard W. Labaree et al., eds., *The Papers of Benjamin Franklin* (New Haven, Conn.: Yale University Press, 1959–), 21:86 (hereafter PBF).

2. BF to Thomas Cushing, January 5, 1774, ibid., 21:6.

3. The Preliminary Hearing before the Privy Council Committee for Plantation Affairs, ibid. 21.

4. Ibid., 23.

5. BF to Jane Mecom, November 1, 1773, PBF 20:457.

6. *Pennsylvania Gazette*, April 20, 1774, PBF 21:112.

7. BF to Thomas Cushing, February 15, 1774, to Joseph Galloway (hereafter JG), February 18, 1774, ibid., 90, 109.

8. Herbert Butterfield, *George III, Lord North, and the People, 1779–1780* (London: G. Bell and Sons, 1949), 36.

9. George III to Lord North, February 23, 1775, in John Fortescue, ed., *The Correspondence of King George III* (London: Macmillan, 1928), 3:181; King George III to John Robinson, June 6, 1779, in Bonamy Dobree, ed., *The Letters of King George III* (New York: Funk & Wagnalls, 1935), 130.

10. Alan Valentine, *Lord North* (Norman: University of Oklahoma Press, 1977), 223, 289.

11. General Gage to Thomas Hutchinson, February 2, 1774, in Thomas Hutchinson, *The Diary and Letters of His Excellency Thomas Hutchinson, Esq.* (Boston: Houghton Mifflin, 1884–86), 1:99; BF to Thomas Cushing, February 15, 1774, PBF 21:92.

12. General Gage to Thomas Hutchinson, February 2, 1774, Hutchinson, *Diary and Letters*, 1:99; BF to Thomas Cushing, February 15, 1774, PBF 21:91.

13. General Gage to Thomas Hutchinson, February 2, 1774, Hutchinson, *Diary and Letters*, 1:100.

14. Ibid., 99; The Final Hearing Before the Privy Council Committee for Plantation Affairs on the Petition from the Massachusetts House of Representatives for the Removal of Hutchinson and Oliver, January 29, 1774, PBF 21:43, 44.

15. Final Hearing, PBF 21:47–49, 53, 56, 58, 65.

16. Ibid., 55.

17. William Bollan to the Massachusetts Council, n.d., PBF 21:40n.

18. PBF 21:41; *Public Advertiser*, February 2, 1774, ibid., 40n.

19. BF to Thomas Cushing, February 15, 1774, 92; *Pennsylvania Gazette*, April 20, 1774, PBF 21:113.

20. Final Hearing, PBF 21:68.

21. The Report of the Privy Council, Committee at the Council Chamber, Whitehall, January 29, 1774, PBF 21:70.

22. BF to Thomas Cushing, January 5, 1773; BF to JG, February 14, 1773, PBF 20:9, 65.

23. BF to JG, November 3, 1773, PBF 20:462.

24. BF to the Massachusetts House Committee of Correspondence, February 2, 1774, PBF 21:74.

25. BF to Thomas Cushing, March 22, 1774, ibid., 153.

26. Ibid., 152.

27. BF, "An Open Letter to Lord Buckinghamshire," *Public Advertiser*, April 2, 1774, ibid., 178.

28. BF to Thomas Cushing, July 7, 1773, PBF 20:272.

29. BF to Thomas Cushing, December 2, 1772, PBF 19:411.

30. BF to JG, February 18, 1774, PBF 21:109.

31. BF to Thomas Cushing, December 2, 1772, PBF 19:411–413.

32. BF to Thomas Cushing, February 15[–19?], 1774, PBF 21:93.

33. BF to JG, February 18, 1774; Tract Relative to the Affair of Hutchinson's Letters, ibid., 110, 430.

34. BF to Thomas Cushing, February 15, 1774, ibid., 86.

35. *The Craftsmen*, January 1, 1774, in Hutchinson, *Diary and Letters*, 91.

36. BF to Thomas Cushing, February 15, 1774, PBF 21:90.

37. *Morning Post*, January 16, 1774, in Hutchinson, *Diary and Letters*, 92; BF to Thomas Cushing, January 5, 1774, PBF 21:7.

38. The Report of the Privy Council Committee, January 29, 1774, ibid., 70.

39. Final Hearing, ibid., 55.

40. Hutchinson, *Diary and Letters*, 157, 159.

41. Thomas Hutchinson to Thomas Hutchinson Jr., July 6, 1774, ibid., 180.

42. See, e.g., diary entries for July 16, August 3–6 in ibid., 192, 204, 208.

43. Ibid., 209, 210.

44. Ibid., 221, 222.

45. Ibid., 232, 245.

46. Ibid., 353.

47. Thomas Hutchinson to Mr. Green, January 10, 1775, ibid., 356.

48. Ibid., 185.

49. Thomas Hutchinson to General Gage, July 4, 1774, ibid., 167, 177.

50. Thomas Hutchinson to Thomas Hutchinson Jr., July 6, 1774, ibid., 179.

51. George III to Lord North, July 1, 1774, in Fortescue, *Correspondence*, 116.

52. Hutchinson, *Diary and Letters*, 261.

53. Thomas Hutchinson to Thomas Hutchinson Jr., January 9, 1775, ibid., 352.

54. Thomas Hutchinson to [?] Pepperell, August 15, 1774, ibid., 128.

55. Ibid., 163.

56. Ibid., 232; Thomas Hutchinson to [?], February 9, 1775, to Peter Oliver, March 24, 1775, ibid., 390, 411. The spelling in this quote has been modernized for purposes of clarity. In most instances, the eighteenth-century spelling will be retained. On occasion the text will depart from the original construction.

57. Thomas Hutchinson to Mr. Green, January 10, 1775, ibid., 356.

58. Ibid., 322.

59. Ibid., 219.

60. *Pennsylvania Gazette*, April 20, 1774, PBF 21:114.

61. BF to Thomas Cushing, February 15, 1774, to Jane Mecom, February 17, 1774, to JG, February 18, 1774, ibid., 94, 103, 109.

62. BF to the *Public Ledger* [March 9, 1774], ibid., 134.

63. Ibid., 13–18.

64. BF, Tract Relative to the Hutchinson Letters [1774], ibid., 414.

65. Hutchinson, *Diary and Letters*, 420, 421.

66. BF to William Franklin (hereafter WF), March 22, 1775, PBF 21:546.

67. Benjamin Franklin, *The Autobiography of Benjamin Franklin*, ed. Leonard W. Labaree et al. (New Haven, Conn.: Yale University Press, 1964), 76.

68. Ibid., 110, 111, 126.

Chapter 2

1. Samuel Cooper to Benjamin Franklin (hereafter BF), July 10, 1771, in Leonard W. Labaree etal., eds., *The Papers of Benjamin Franklin* (New Haven, Conn.: Yale University Press, 1959--) PBF 18:172 (hereafter PBF).

2. BF to William Franklin (hereafter WF), July 2, 1768, PBF 15:163.

3. Ian R. Christie, *Wars and Revolutions: Britain, 1760–1815* (Cambridge, Mass.: Harvard University Press, 1982), 74; BF to Joseph Galloway (hereafter JG), January 9, 1769, PBF 15:16.

4. Lord Hillsborough to the Governors in America, April 21, 1768, in Frederick W. Ricord and William Nelson, eds., *Documents Relating to the Colonial History of the State of New Jersey* (Newark, N.J.: Daily Advertiser Printing House, 1886), 10:14, 15 (hereafter NJA).

5. Carolyn Smith Knapp, "The British Response to the Idea of American Independence, 1607–1815," Ph.D. dissertation, University of California, Berkeley, 95.

6. BF to Dennys DeBerdt, August 31, 1768, PBF 15:197.

7. PBF 17:257, 258.

8. BF to [?], January 16, 1771, PBF 18:9–16.

9. BF to Thomas Cushing, February 5, 1771, ibid., 28.

10. Lord Hillsborough to General Gage, April 15, 1768, in Clarence E. Carter, *The Correspondence of General Thomas Gage* (New Haven, Conn.: Yale University Press, 1931), 2:62.

11. BF to WF, [September 27, 1766], PBF 13:425.

12. Lord Hillsborough to General Gage, July 31, 1770, in Carter, *Correspondence*, 2:108.

13. See Clarence Walworth Alvord, *The Mississippi Valley in British Politics: A Study of the Trade, Land Speculation, and Experiments in Imperialism Culminating in the American Revolution* (Cleveland: Arthur H. Clark, 1917), 2:23, 24, 42, 43, 51.

14. Colin G. Calloway, *The Scratch of a Pen: 1763 and the Transformation of North America* (New York: Oxford University Press, 2006), 60.

15. WF to BF, April 30, 1766, PBF 13:257.

16. BF to WF, [June 13, 1767], PBF 14:180.

17. BF to WF, April 20, 1771, PBF 18:76.

18. BF to Thomas Cushing, June 10, 1771, ibid., 122.

19. Edmund Burke to James DeLancey, August 20, 1772, in Lucy S. Sutherland, ed., *Correspondence of Edmund Burke* (Chicago: University of Chicago Press, 1960), 2:327.

20. Alan Valentine, *Lord North* (Norman: University of Oklahoma Press, 1977), 25; Herbert Butterfield, *George III, Lord North, and the People, 1779–1780* (London: G. Bell and Sons, 1949), 22, 23; Peter D. G. Thomas, *Lord North* (New York: St. Martin's Press, 1976), 5; Edmund Burke to Charles O'Hara, [May 22, 1773], in Sutherland, *Correspondence*, 2:434.

21. Thomas Hutchinson, *The Diary and Letters of His Excellency Thomas Hutchinson, Esq.* (Boston: Houghton Mifflin, 1884–1886), 444.

22. Ibid., 398.

23. Valentine, *Lord North*, 190, 191.

24. Ibid., 25; Thomas, *Lord North*, 9, 41–43; Butterfield, *King George III*, 22, 23; Alvord, *Mississippi Valley*.

25. Thomas, *Lord North*, 222; Valentine, *Lord North*, 137, 154, 157.

26. BF to WF, January 9, 1768, PBF 15:16.

27. BF to WF, April 16, 1768, ibid., 98, 99.

28. Valentine, *Lord North*, 232, 235.

29. Ibid., 129, 175, 199, 200; Thomas, *Lord North*, 15, 16.

30. BF to Thomas Cushing, June 4, 1773, PBF 20:228.

31. Benjamin Franklin, *The Autobiography of Benjamin Franklin*, ed. Leonard W. Labaree et al. (New Haven, Conn.: Yale University Press, 1964), 223 (hereafter *Autobiography*).

32. John Richard Alden, *General Gage in America, Being Principally a History of His Role in the American Revolution* (Baton Rouge: Louisiana State University Press, 1948), 102, 103.

33. David Hackett Fischer, *Paul Revere's Ride* (New York: Oxford University Press, 1994), 34, 35.

34. George Croghan to BF, January 27, 1767, PBF 14:12.

35. General Gage to Viscount Barrington, August 6, 1771, in Carter, *Correspondence*, 2:587.

36. Alden, *General Gage in America*, 149.

37. General Gage to Viscount Barrington, May 14, 1759, in Carter, *Correspondence*, 2:510.

38. General Gage to Viscount Barrington, January 16, 1766, ibid., 334.

39. General Gage to Viscount Barrington, February 4, 1769, ibid., 499.

40. General Gage to Viscount Barrington, July 22, October 7, 1769, ibid., 518, 527.

41. BF to Samuel Cooper, June 8, 1770, PBF 17:162.

42. General Gage to Viscount Barrington, July 6, 1770, in Carter, *Correspondence*, 2:546, 547. See BF to JG, March 21, 1770, to Samuel Cooper, June 8, 1770, PBF 17:117, 165.

43. BF to JG, June 11, 1770, PBF 17:169.

44. Ibid., 170.

45. General Gage to Viscount Barrington, November 6, 1771, in Carter, *Correspondence*, 2:592.

46. General Gage to Viscount Barrington, February 8, 1773, ibid., 636.

47. ibid.

48. Edmund Burke to General Charles Lee, February 1, 1774, to the Marquess of Rockingham, February 2, 1774, in Sutherland, *Correspondence*, 2:518, 724.

49. Edmund Burke to the Committee of Correspondence of the General Assembly of New York, February 2, 1774, ibid., 522.

50. Edmund Burke to General Charles Lee, February 1, 1774, to the Committee of Correspondence of the General Assembly of New York, February 2, 1774, ibid., 518, 521.

51. See W. J. Bate, ed., *Edmund Burke: Selected Works* (New York: Modern Library, 1960, 13); R. J. White, *The Age of George III* (New York: Doubleday, 1969), 104, 105; Richard Pares, *King George III and the Politicians* (Oxford: Clarendon Press, 1953), 100.

52. Sutherland, *Correspondence*, 2:xv.

53. Edmund Burke to the Committee of Correspondence of the General Assembly of New York, December 4, 1771, to James DeLancey, December 4, 1771, ibid., 290, 291, 293.

54. Elliott Robert Barkan, ed., *Edmund Burke on the American Revolution: Selected Speeches and Letters* (Gloucester, Mass.: Peter Smith, 1972), xii.

55. Hutchinson, *Diary and Letters*, 1:359, 361.

56. Burke, "Speech Introducing a Motion for an Enquiry into the Causes of the Late Disorders in America, May 9, 1770," in Barkan, *Edmund Burke*, 9.

57. Burke, "Speech Before the House of Commons in Support of Rose Fuller's Motion that the Commons Move to a Committee of the Whole in Order to Discuss the Three Pence Tax on Tea," April 19, 1774, ibid., 39.

58. Ibid., 65; Burke, "Speech in Support of Resolutions for Conciliation with the American Colonies," March 22, 1775, ibid., 109.

59. Burke, "Speech in Support of Resolutions for Conciliation," ibid., 73, 75, 91.

60. Barkan, *Burke*, xv, xv1; C. B. MacPherson, *Burke* (New York: Hill & Wang, 1980), 15, 27.

61. Bernard Bailyn, *The Ordeal of Thomas Hutchinson* (Cambridge, Mass.: Harvard University Press, 1974), 20.

62. *Autobiography*, 145.

63. Thomas Hutchinson to [?], August 8, 1774, to Mr. Isaac Bigelo [?] August 1774, to Sally Hutchinson Oliver, November 1, 1774, Hutchinson, *Diary and Letters* 215, 231, 281.

64. Bailyn, *Ordeal*, 28–31.

Chapter 3

1. Benjamin Franklin, *The Autobiography of Benjamin Franklin*, ed. Leonard W. Labaree et al. (New Haven, Conn.: Yale University Press, 1964), 43 (hereafter *Autobiography*).

2. Ibid., 69.

3. Ibid., 80.

4. Ibid., 82.

5. Ibid., 95.

6. Ibid., 96.

7. Ibid., 92.

8. Ibid., 129.

9. Ibid., 128.

10. Ibid.

11. Ibid., 129.

12. See Gordon S. Wood, *The Americanization of Benjamin Franklin* (New York: Penguin, 2004), 51–54, for a full rundown of Franklin's business ventures.

13. *Autobiography*, 197.

14. Benjamin Franklin (hereafter BF) to William Johnson, August 11, 1755, to Richard Partridge, November 27, 1755, in Leonard W. Labaree et al., eds., *The Papers of Benjamin Franklin* (New Haven, Conn.: Yale University Press, 1959–), 6:140, 274 (hereafter PBF).

15. William Strahan to Deborah Franklin, December 13, 1757, PBF 7:297.

16. *Autobiography*, 159.

17. Ibid., 261, 262.

18. BF to [Isaac Norris?], January 14, 1758, PBF 7:362.

19. BF to Joseph Galloway (hereafter JG), February 17, 1758, ibid., 374.

20. Benjamin H. Newcomb, *Franklin and Galloway: A Political Partnership* (New Haven, Conn.: Yale University Press, 1972), 67.

21. Franklin, *A Narrative of the Late Massacres*, PBF 11:68.

22. See Lorett Treese, *The Storm Gathering: The Penn Family and the American Revolution* (University Park: Pennsylvania State University Press, 1992), 38–42.

23. BF to John Fothergill, March 14, 1764, ibid., 103, 104.

24. BF to Richard Jackson, February 11, 1764, ibid., 78.

25. BF to Henry Bouquet, September 30, 1764, ibid., 367.

26. Franklin, *Cool Thoughts on the Present Situation of Public Affairs*, ibid., 171.

27. BF to Richard Jackson, September 1, 1764, ibid., 329.

28. BF to William Strahan, September 1, 1764, ibid., 332.

29. Pennsylvania Assembly, *Instructions to Richard Jackson*, September 22, 1764, ibid., 348.

30. BF to Richard Jackson, February 11, 1764, ibid., 76.

31. BF to Charles Thomson, July 11, 1765, PBF 12:207.

32. BF to Richard Jackson, February 11, 1764, PBF 11:76.

33. BF to Charles Thomson, [September 24, 1765], PBF 12:278, 279.

34. BF to Josiah Tucker, February 26, 1774, PBF 21:126.

35. David Hall to BF, October 14, 1765, PBF 12:320.

36. BF to John Hughes, August 9, 1765, ibid., 234, 235.

37. Thomas Hutchinson, *The Diary and Letters of His Excellency Thomas Hutchinson, Esq.* (Boston: Houghton Mifflin, 1884–1886), 70.

38. BF to David Hall, September 14, 1765, PBF 12:267.

39. JG to BF, September 20, 1765, ibid., 269.

40. P. Langford, *The First Rockingham Administration, 1765–1766* (London: Oxford University Press, 1973), 100.

41. BF to William Franklin (hereafter WF), November 9, 1765, ibid., 365.

42. BF to Lord Kames, February 25, 1767, PBF 14:64.

43. BF to David Hall, November 9, 1765, PBF 12:365, 366.

44. BF to William Strahan, [January 14, 1766], PBF 13:41–43.

45. BF to Richard Jackson, September 25, 1764, PBF 11:359.

46. Examination before the Committee of the Whole of the House of Commons, 1766, PBF 13:140.

47. Ibid., 134.

48. Ibid., 135.

49. Ibid., 150.

50. Ibid., 136.

51. Ibid., 142.

52. Ibid., 145.

53. Ibid., 139.

54. BF to WF, March 13, 1768, PBF 15:76.

55. BF to Joseph Fox, February 24, 1766, to David Hall, February 24, 1766, PBF 13:168–170.

56. JG to BF, June 7, 1766, ibid., 295.

57. Quoted in ibid., 125n.

58. See, for instance, Charles Thomson to BF, May 20, 1766, JG to BF, May 23, June 7, 1766, ibid., 278, 285, 295.

59. BF to David Hall, February 24, 1766, ibid., 170.

60. Examination Before the Commons, ibid., 141.

61. BF to Joseph Fox, March 1, 1766, ibid., 186, 187.

62. BF to the Pennsylvania Assembly Committee of Correspondence, June 10, 1766, ibid., 299.

63. Thomas Wharton to BF, May 22, 1766, ibid., 282.

64. Franklin, "Benevolus," printed in the *London Chronicle*, April 8–11, 1767, PBF 14:114.

65. See, for example, PBF 15:241–244.

66. BF to WF, March 13, 1768, ibid., 75, 76.

67. BF to [Charles Thomson], March 18, 1770, PBF 17:111.

68. BF to Humphry Marshall, March 18, 1770, ibid., 109, 110.

69. BF to JG, March 21, 1770, ibid., 117.

70. BF to [Charles Thomson], March 18, 1770, to JG, March 21, 1770, ibid., 111, 115.

71. King George III to Thomas Hutchinson, July 1, 1774, in Bonamy Dobree, ed., *The Letters of King George III* (New York: Funk & Wagnalls, 1935), 104.

72. Thomas Hutchinson to General Gage, October 20, 1774, to [?]. February 29, 1775, in Hutchinson, *Diary and Letters*, 266, 390.

Chapter 4

1. Benjamin Franklin (hereafter BF) to [?], November 28, 1768, in Leonard W. Labaree et al., eds., *The Papers of Benjamin Franklin* (New Haven, Conn.: Yale University Press, 1959–), 15:273 (hereafter PBF).

2. BF to Joseph Galloway (hereafter JG), January 9, 1768, ibid., 17.

3. Bernard Bailyn, *Ideological Origins of the American Revolution* (Cambridge, Mass.: Belknap Press of Harvard University Press, 1967), 153.

4. Quoted in ibid., 56.

5. George III to George Grenville, February 18, 1764, to Viscount Weymouth, May 10, 1768, in Bonamy Dobree, ed., *The Letters of King George III* (New York: Funk & Wagnalls, 1935), 27, 53.

6. Fred Anderson, *A People's Army: Massachusetts Soldiers and Society in the Seven Years War* (New York: W. W. Norton, 1984), 176, 177.

7. General Gage to Viscount Barrington, November 8, 1768, in Clarence E. Carter, *The Correspondence of General Thomas Gage* (New Haven, Conn.: Yale University Press, 1931), 2:491.

8. General Gage to Viscount Barrington, February 4, May 14, 1769, ibid., 499, 509.

9. Governor Francis Bernard to Viscount Barrington, November 23, 1765, in Edward Channing and Archibald Cary Coolidge, eds., *The Barrington-Bernard Correspondence and Illustrative Matter, 1760–1770* (Cambridge, Mass.: Harvard University Press, 1912), 95.

10. Quoted in Paul David Nelson, *William Tryon and the Course of Empire: A Life in British Imperial Service* (Chapel Hill: University of North Carolina Press, 1990), 68.

11. William Franklin (hereafter WF) to Lord Dartmouth, August 2, 1775, in Frederick W. Ricord and William Nelson, eds., *Documents Relating to the Colonial History of the State of New Jersey* (Newark, N.J.: Daily Advertiser Printing House, 1886), 10:653 (hereafter NJA).

12. See Thomas Moffatt, *Account of the Newport Riots in August 1765*, Chalmers Papers Relating to Rhode Island, 1637–1785, New York Public Library, New York (hereafter Chalmers Papers); Thomas Moffatt to Joseph Harrison, October 16, 1765, Chalmers Papers; Martin Howard Jr., "A Letter from a Gentleman at Halifax, 1765," in Merrill Jensen, ed., *Tracts of the American Revolution, 1763–1776* (Indianapolis: Bobbs-Merrill, 1967), 73; *Newport Mercury*, April 23, 1764.

13. Governor Bernard to Viscount Barrington, November 23, 1765, in Channing and Coolidge, *Barrington-Bernard Correspondence*, 97, 98.

14. Governor Bernard to Viscount Barrington, May 30, July 8, 1769, ibid., 203, 206.

15. General Gage to Viscount Barrington, January 17, 1766, in Carter, *Correspondence*, 2:406.

16. General Gage to Viscount Barrington, June 28, 1768, ibid., 479, 480.

17. Ian Christie, *Wars and Revolutions: Britain 1760–1815* (Cambridge, Mass.: Harvard University, 1982), 64.

18. See especially Geoffrey Holmes and Daniel Szechi, *The Age of Oligarchy: Pre-Industrial Britain, 1722–1783* (New York: Longman, 1993), 292, 293.

19. Burke, "Thoughts on the Cause of the Present Discontents, 1770," in David Womersly, ed., *A Philosophical Enquiry into the Origin of Our Ideas of the Sublime and Beautiful, and Other Pre-Revolutionary Writings* (New York: Penguin, 1998), 213.

20. Burke, "Letter to the Sheriffs of Bristol, 1777," in W. J. Bate, ed., *Edmund Burke: Selected Works* (New York: Modern Library, 1960), 194, 223.

21. Burke, "Thoughts," 214, 215.

22. Ibid., 224.

23. Ibid., 230, 248.

24. R. J. White, *The Age of George III* (New York: Doubleday, 1969), 93.

25. James Otis, "The Rights of the British Colonies Asserted and Proved, 1764," in Jensen, *Tracts of the Revolution*, 28.

26. George III to Lieutenant-General Conway, [December 5, 1765], in Dobree, *George III*, 33, 34.

27. "The Lords' Protests," 1766, PBF 13:220, 221.

28. BF to JG, December 1, 1767, PBF 14:329.

29. Anon, "A Letter to the Right Honourable Frederick, Lord North," 1774, quoted in Carolyn Smith Knapp, "The British Response to the Idea of American Independence, 1607–1815," Ph.D. dissertation, University of California, Berkeley, 107.

30. George III to Lord North, September 11, 1774, in Dobree, *George III*, 105.

31. Hutchinson, *Diary and Letters*, 367.

32. Ibid.

33. Ibid., 423.

34. Ibid., 342, 359.

35. Ibid., 297.

36. Ibid., 355.

37. Ibid., 297; Thomas Hutchinson to Mr. Erving, March 10, 1775, Ibid., 401.

38. Thomas Hutchinson to Peter Oliver, March 24, 1775, Ibid., 405.

39. Ibid., 405.

40. Ibid., 185, 340.

41. Tract Relative to the Affair of Hutchinson's Letters, [1774], PBF 21:419.

42. BF to JG, June 13, 1767, PBF 14:184.

43. BF to William Strahan, August 8, 1763, PBF 10:320.

44. BF to Mary Stevenson, March 25, 1763, ibid., 232.

45. BF to William Shirley, December 22, 1754, PBF 5:450.

46. BF to Lord Kames, June 3, 1760, PBF 9:7.

47. BF to John Whitehurst, June 27, 1763, to William Strahan, December 19, 1763, PBF 10:302, 407.

48. BF to Samuel Cooper, June 8, 1770, PBF 17:163.

49. BF, "On the Candidacy of Barlow Threthick," *The Pennsylvania Chronicle, and Universal Adviser*, December 5–12, 1768, PBF 15:67.

50. BF to Samuel Cooper, June 8, 1770, PBF 17:162, 164.

51. BF to the Massachusetts House of Representatives, July 7, 1773, PBF 20:283.

52. BF to Thomas Cushing, February 5, 1771, PBF 18:27.

53. BF to JG, August 8, 1767, July 2, 1768, PBF 14:228, 15:164.

54. BF to Jonathan Williams Sr., June 6, 1770, PBF 17:157.

55. BF to WF, November 9, 1765, PBF 12:360.

56. BF to WF, August 17, 1772, to Thomas Cushing, November 4, 1772, PBF 19:244, 364.

57. BF to WF, July 14, 1773, PBF 20:308.

58. Brendan McConville, *The King's Three Faces: The Rise and Fall of Royal America, 1688–1776* (Chapel Hill: University of North Carolina Press, 2006), 121.

59. BF to Thomas Cushing, February 15–19, 1774, PBF 21:93, 94.

60. BF to JG, February 18, 1774, BF, "Tract Relative to the Affair of Hutchinson's Letters," ibid., 110, 430.

61. BF to Thomas Cushing, February 15–19, 1774, ibid., 91, 92.

62. BF to Peter Collinson, May 9, 1753, PBF 4:486.

63. BF to JG, February 17, 1758, PBF 7:375.

64. BF to Thomas Cushing, October 10, 1774, PBF 21:329.

65. To *The Public Ledger* [after March 9, 1774], ibid., 134, 135.

66. BF to JG, February 25, 1775, ibid., 509.

67. BF to *The Public Ledger* [after March 9, 1774], ibid., 137, 138.

68. BF to Jonathan Williams Sr., September 28, 1774, ibid., 323, 324.

69. BF to WF, March 22, 1775, ibid., 551.

Chapter 5

1. Benjamin Franklin (hereafter BF) to William Franklin (hereafter WF), February 2, 1774, in Leonard W. Labaree et al., eds., *The Papers of Benjamin Franklin* (New Haven, Conn.: Yale University Press, 1959–), 21:75 (hereafter PBF).

2. BF to WF, February 18, 1774, ibid., 107, 108.

3. BF to WF, May 7, 1774, ibid., 212.

4. Quoted in Sheila L. Skemp, *First Lady of Letters: Judith Sargent Murray and the Struggle for Female Independence* (Philadelphia: University of Pennsylvania Press, 2009), 88, 89.

5. WF to the New Jersey Assembly, June 17, 1776, in Frederick W. Ricord and William Nelson, eds., *Documents Relating to the Colonial History of the State of New Jersey* (Newark, N.J.: Daily Advertiser Printing House, 1886), 10:727, 728 (hereafter NJA).

6. BF to Jane Mecom, [June] 1748, PBF 3:303.

7. BF to William Strahan, October 19, 1748, ibid., 321.

8. William Strahan to Deborah Franklin, December 13, 1757, PBF 7:297.

9. WF to BF, December 24, 1774, PBF 21:402.

10. BF to WF, July 2, 1768, PBF 15:161.

11. BF to John Hughes, August 9, 1765, PBF 12:235.

12. WF to BF, November 13, 1765, ibid., 369.

13. WF to Lord Hillsborough, November 23, 1768, NJA 10:69.

14. Ibid., 70.

15. WF to Lord Dartmouth, January 28, September 6, December 6, 1774, ibid., 465, 474, 504.

16. BF to WF, October 6, 1773, PBF 20:437.

17. BF to WF, September 7, 1774, PBF 21:287.

18. WF to BF, July 29, 1773, PBF 20:332.

19. BF to WF, September 1, 1773, ibid., 287.

20. BF to WF, October 6, 1773, ibid., 439.

21. BF to WF, September 1, 1773, ibid., 387.

22. WF to BF, December 24, 1774, PBF 21:404.

23. WF to Lord Dartmouth, December 6, 1774, NJA 10:570.

24. BF to WF. March 22, 1775, PBF 21:581–583.

25. WF to BF, December 24, 1774, ibid., 404.

26. WF to Lord Dartmouth, August 2, 1775, NJA 10:563.

27. *Votes and Proceedings of the General Assembly of the Province of New Jersey* (Philadelphia: Andrew Bradford, 1775), A5.

28. BF to David Hartley, September 12, 1775, to Jonathan Shipley, September 13, 1775, PBF 22:196, 199.

29. BF to David Hartley, October 3, 1775, ibid., 217.

30. WF to New Jersey Assembly, June 23, 1776, Revolutionary Era MSS, New Jersey Historical Society, Newark, New Jersey.

31. WF to William Temple Franklin, June 3, 1776, Franklin Papers 101:16, American Philosophical Society, Philadelphia, Pennsylvania (hereafter Franklin Papers).

32. *Minutes of the Provincial Congress and the Council of Safety of the State of New Jersey* (Trenton, N.J.: Naar, Day, and Naar, 1879), 454–457.

33. WF to Legislature of New Jersey, June 17, 1776, NJA 10:721.

34. *Minutes of the Provincial Congress*, 470.

35. Ronald Hoffman, "The 'Disaffected' in the Revolutionary South," in Alfred F. Young, ed., *The American Revolution: Explorations in the History of American Radicalism* (DeKalb: Northern Illinois University Press, 1976), 293.

36. WF to BF, July 22, 1784, Franklin Papers, MSS, American Philosophical Society.

37. BF to WF, August 16, 1784, in Albert H. Smyth, ed., *The Writings of Benjamin Franklin* (New York: Macmillan, 1906), 9:252.

38. BF Will, Codicil, June 23, 1789, Franklin Papers, MSS, American Philosophical Society.

39. BF to Lord Howe, July 20, 1776, PBF 22:520.

FOR FURTHER READING
....

Anyone interested in Benjamin Franklin's long and eventful life would do well to begin by letting Franklin speak for himself. Although it was, like all autobiographies, self-serving, his *Autobiography* remains as fascinating a piece of early American literature as it was when Franklin wrote it. Any edition will do. Perhaps the best of the lot is edited by Leonard W. Labaree et al. (New Haven, Conn.: Yale University Press, 1964). Labaree was also the first chief editor of the multivolume *Papers of Benjamin Franklin*, the first volume of which was published by Yale University Press in 1959. Thus far, a succession of editors and their diligent staffs have produced 39 of a projected 47 volumes that include letters to and from Franklin, as well as his published and unpublished work. The volumes are exquisite. They are thorough and beautifully edited. For the period after May 15, 1783, scholars should go to Albert H. Smyth, ed., *The Writings of Benjamin Franklin*, 10 vols. (New York: Macmillan, 1905–1907).

General biographies of Benjamin Franklin abound. Noteworthy in this regard are Edmund S. Morgan, *Benjamin Franklin* (New Haven, Conn.: Yale University Press, 2002); Esmond Wright, *Franklin of Philadelphia* (Cambridge, Mass.: Harvard University Press 1986); Walter Isaacson, *Benjamin Franklin: An American Life* (New York: Simon & Schuster, 2003); and Jonathan R. Dull, *Benjamin Franklin and the American Revolution* (Lincoln: University of Nebraska Press, 2010). For less adulatory perspectives on Franklin, see Robert Middlekauff, *Benjamin Franklin and His Enemies* (Berkeley: University of California Press, 1996); Gordon S. Wood, *The Americanization* of *Benjamin Franklin* (New York: Penguin Press, 2004); and David Waldstreicher, *Runaway America: Benjamin Franklin, Slavery, and the American Revolution* (New York: Hill & Wang, 2004). Readers wanting to know more about Franklin's personal life will find Claude-Anne Lopez and Eugenia Herbert, *The Private Franklin: The Man and His Family* (New York: W. W. Norton, 1975), and Thomas Fleming, *The Man Who Dared the Lightning* (New York: William Morrow, 1971), both enlightening and entertaining.

Franklin's involvement in Pennsylvania politics is both complicated and fascinating. See especially William S. Hanna, *Benjamin Franklin and Pennsylvania Politics* (Stanford, Calif.: Stanford University Press, 1964); James H. Hutson, *Pennsylvania Politics, 1746–1760: The Movement for Royal Government and Its Consequences* (Princeton, N.J.: Princeton University Press, 1972); Benjamin H. Newcomb, *Franklin and Galloway: A Political Partnership* (New Haven, Conn.: Yale University Press, 1962); and Lorett Treese, *The Storm Gathering: The Penn Family and the American Revolution* (University Park: Pennsylvania State University Press, 1992). Those intrigued by Franklin's electoral defeat at the hands of the Proprietary Party could do no better than to read J. Philip Gleason's classic "A Scurrilous Colonial Election and Franklin's Reputation," *William and Mary Quarterly* 18, 3rd ser. (1961): 68–84.

Some scholars have analyzed the political philosophy that informed Franklin's view of Anglo-colonial relations. Most valuable in this regard are Paul W. Conner's *Poor Richard's Politicks: Benjamin Franklin and His New American Order* (New York: Oxford University Press, 1965) and Lorraine Smith Pangle's *The Political Philosophy of Benjamin Franklin* (Baltimore: Johns Hopkins University Press, 2007). Ormond Seavy, *Becoming Benjamin Franklin: The Autobiography and the Life* (Philadelphia: University of Pennsylvania Press, 1988), is also useful. Franklin's experience as a colonial agent was instrumental in helping him develop his changing views of empire. See especially Michael J. Kammen, *A Rope of Sand: The Colonial Agents, British Politics and the American Revolution* (Ithaca, N.Y.: Cornell University Press, 1968), and David T. Morgan, *The Devious Dr. Franklin, Colonial Agent: Benjamin Franklin's Years in London* (Macon, Ga.: Mercer University Press, 1996). For a readable and iconoclastic view of Franklin's London years see Cecil B. Currey, *Road to Revolution: Benjamin Franklin in England, 1765–1775* (New York: Peter Smith, 1968).

Benjamin Franklin spent a great deal of time and energy promoting his various projects for land speculation in what then counted as the American frontier. To appreciate the complexities of his machinations, readers should begin with Clarence Walworth Alvord, *The Mississippi Valley in British Politics: A Study of the Trade, Land Speculation, and Experiments in Imperialism Culminating in the American Revolution* (Cleveland: Arthur H. Clark, 1917). Also useful are Jack M. Sosin's *Whitehall and the Wilderness: The Middle West in British Colonial Policy, 1760–1777* (Lincoln: University of Nebraska Press, 1961) and Peter Marshall's "Lord Hillsborough, Samuel Wharton and the Ohio Grant," *English Historical Review* 80 (1965): 717–739.

Franklin had to deal with an ever-changing—and often hostile—personal and political environment so long as he remained in London. General works looking at eighteenth-century English politics with a focus on Anglo-American relations include Linda Colley, *Britons: Forging the Nation, 1707–1837* (New Haven, Conn.: Yale University Press, 1992); Robert W. Tucker and David C. Hendrickson, *The Fall of the First British Empire: Origin of the War for American Independence* (Baltimore: Johns Hopkins University Press, 1982); Ian R. Christie and Benjamin W. Labaree, *Empire or Independence, 1760–1776: A British Dialogue on the Coming of the American Revolution* (New York: Norton, 1976); Alison Gilbert Olson, *Anglo-American Politics, 1660–1775: The Relationship between Parties in England and Colonial America* (London: Oxford University Press, 1973); Peter Marshall and Glyn Williams, eds., *The British Atlantic Empire before the Revolution* (London: Routledge, 1980); Eliga H. Gould, *The Persistence of Empire: British Political Culture in the Age of the American Revolution* (Chapel Hill: University of North Carolina Press, 2000); and P. Langford, *The First Rockingham Administration, 1765–1766* (London: Oxford University Press, 1973). A few particularly accessible biographies of English notables include Jeremy Black, *George III: America's Last King* (New Haven, Conn.: Yale University Press, 2006); Peter D. G. Thomas, *Lord North* (New York: St. Martin's Press, 1976); Alan Valentine, *Lord North* (Norman: University of Oklahoma Press, 1967); and John Richard Alden, *General Gage in America being Principally a History of His Role in the American Revolution* (Baton Rouge: Louisiana State University Press, 1948).

While most scholars concede that his Cockpit experience was a turning point for Franklin in terms of altering his views of England, William B. Willcox's "Franklin's Last Years in England: The Making of a Rebel," in Melvin H. Buxbaum, ed., *Critical Essays on Benjamin Franklin* (Boston: G. K. Hall, 1987), 96–110, disagrees. The best argument for the significance of the Cockpit remains Jack P. Greene's illuminating "The Alienation of Benjamin Franklin, British American," *Journal of the Royal Society for the Encouragement of the Arts, Manufactures, and Commerce* 124 (1976): 52–73.

For Franklin's relationship with his loyalist son, see Sheila L. Skemp, *Benjamin and William Franklin: Father and Son, Patriot and Loyalist* (Boston: Bedford Books of St. Martin's Press, 1994), and Willard Sterne Randall, *A Little Revenge: Benjamin Franklin and His Son* (Boston: Little, Brown, 1984). For a deeper analysis of William Franklin, see Skemp, *William Franklin: Son of a Patriot, Servant of a King* (New York: Oxford University Press, 1990).

Readers interested in Franklin's role as a minister plenipotentiary in Paris should begin with Jonathan R. Dull, *Franklin the Diplomat: The French Mission* (Philadelphia: American Philosophical Society, 1982); Stacy Schiff, *A Great Improvisation: Franklin, France, and the Birth of America* (New York: Henry Holt, 2005); and Claude-Anne Lopez, *Mon Cher Papa: Franklin and the Ladies of Paris* (New Haven, Conn.: Yale University Press, 1962).

Of course anyone who is interested in Benjamin Franklin is no doubt curious about the American Revolution and its causes as well. A few suggestions will suffice. For a persuasive argument concerning the importance of "conspiracy theory" in the coming of the Revolution, two books in particular stand out: Bernard Bailyn, *Ideological Origins of the American Revolution* (Cambridge, Mass.: Harvard University Press, 1967), and Pauline Maier, *From Resistance to Revolution: Colonial Radicals and the Development of American Opposition to Britain, 1765–1776* (New York: Vintage, 1972). Bailyn's *The Ordeal of Thomas Hutchinson* (Cambridge, Mass.: Harvard University Press, 1974) shows how one man's experience was informed by the sometimes irrational fears that permeated the British Empire in the mid-eighteenth century. Brendan McConville, in his *The King's Three Faces: The Rise and Fall of Royal America, 1688–1776* (Chapel Hill: University of North Carolina Press, 2006), reminds readers that virtually all colonists were staunch royalists at least until 1774. Those who would like to know a little more about the lives and perspectives of colonists who did not rub shoulders with the elite should consult Gary Nash, *The Urban Crucible: Social Change, Political Consciousness, and the Origins of the American Revolution* (Cambridge, Mass.: Harvard University Press, 1979); Nash, *The Unknown American Revolution: The Unruly Birth of Democracy and the Struggle to Create America* (New York: Viking Press, 2005); and Alfred F. Young, *Liberty Tree: Ordinary People and the American Revolution* (New York: New York University Press, 2006).

Some moments in the period between 1763 and 1774 are especially crucial. The significance to Anglo-colonial relations of the French and Indian War cannot be exaggerated. See Fred Anderson, *The War That Made America: A Short History of the French and Indian War* (New York: Penguin, 2006), and Colin G. Calloway, *The Scratch of a Pen: 1763 and the Transformation of North America* (New York: Oxford University Press, 2006). No book offers a more complete examination of the Stamp Act and its ramifications than Edmund S. Morgan and Helen Morgan, *The Stamp Act Crisis: Prologue to Revolution* (Chapel Hill: University of North Carolina Press, 1953).

The "Boston Massacre" continues to be a source of fascination. Although it takes a decidedly jaundiced view of the Boston "mob," Hiller B. Zobel's *The Boston Massacre* (New York: W. W. Norton, 1970) offers a thorough overview of the events of March 5, 1770. Also excellent are Richard Archer, *As If an Enemy's Country: The British Occupation of Boston and the Origins of the Revolution* (New York: Oxford University Press, 2010), and Neil L. York, *The Boston Massacre: A History with Documents* (London: Routledge, 2010). Benjamin Woods Labaree's *The Boston Tea Party* (Boston: Northeastern University Press, 1964) gives a lively account of the events leading up to the destruction of the tea in Boston Harbor in 1773. See also Benjamin L. Carp, *Defiance of the Patriots: The Boston Tea Party and the Making of America* (New Haven, Conn.: Yale University Press, 2010). For the perspective of Bostonians actually involved in the "tea party," see especially Alfred F. Young, *The Shoemaker and the Tea Party: Memory and the American Revolution* (Boston: Beacon Press, 1999).

The sufferings of loyal Americans have been noted by many historians. Of particular note are Robert M. Calhoon, *The Loyalists in Revolutionary America: 1760–1781* (New York: Harcourt Brace Jovanovich, 1973), and his *The Loyalist Perception and Other Essays* (Columbia: University of South Carolina Press, 1989). Ronald Hoffman's "The 'Disaffected' in the Revolutionary South," in Alfred F. Young, ed., *The American Revolution: Explorations in the History of American Radicalism* (DeKalb: University of Northern Illinois Press, 1976), explicitly characterizes the American Revolution as a civil war. T. H. Breen's *American Insurgents, American Patriots: The Revolution of the People* (New York: Hill & Wang, 2010) argues that Patriots perpetrated few atrocities and that while every colony experienced divisions, the people who encountered the king's supporters were generally moderate and strove to give due process to their opponents.

INDEX

....

Note: Page numbers in *italics* indicate illustrations.

Adams, John, 111–112
Adams, Samuel, 13, 101, 113, 152
agents, colonial, 2, 8, 32
Albany Conference (1754), 57, 67,
　121, 129
Alden, John Richard, 173
Alexander, William, 142
Alvord, Clarence Walworth, 173
American Philosophical Society, 65
Amherst, Jeffrey, 46, 73, 101
Anderson, Fred, 174
Archer, Richard, 175
Aristotle, 99
Austrian Succession, War of
　(1740–1748), 129
Autobiography (Franklin), 26–27,
　45, 171
　his life's "errata" in, 59–62, 64,
　　66–67, 94, 156

Bailyn, Bernard, 174
Barclay, David, 124

Barry, James, *51*
Bentham, Jeremy, 2
Bernard, Francis, 15, 31, 101–103,
　118, 136, 155
Beverley, Robert, 127
Black, Jeremy, 173
Bloomsbury Gang, 38
Boston Massacre (1770), 17, 42,
　110–112, 175
Boston Tea Party (1773), 3–5, 12,
　103, 112
　causes of, 8–9
　Franklin on, 13–14, 155
Braddock, Edward, 45, 130
Breen, T. H., 175
Brown, Mather, *130*
Burke, Edmund, 2, 29, 30, 50–55,
　92, 94
　on Lord Hillsborough, 38
　Hutchinson on, 95
　on Lord North, 39
　on parliamentary power,
　　104–105, 109, 155